CSS Mastery: Styling Web Pages Like a Pro

Kameron Hussain and Frahaan Hussain

Published by Sonar Publishing, 2023.

While every precaution has been taken in the preparation of this book, the publisher assumes no responsibility for errors or omissions, or for damages resulting from the use of the information contained herein.

CSS MASTERY: STYLING WEB PAGES LIKE A PRO

First edition. November 12, 2023.

ISBN: 979-8223825807

Written by Kameron Hussain and Frahaan Hussain.

Table of Contents

1. Minification

2. CSS Compression

3. Remove Unused Code

4. Combine CSS Files

5. Optimize Images in CSS

6. Use CSS Sprites

7. Avoid @import

8. Media Queries and Conditional Loading

9. Caching

10. Content Delivery Networks (CDNs)

Section 14.2: Minification and Compression

1. Minification

2. Compression

Section 14.3: Critical CSS for Faster Page Loading

1. Understanding Critical CSS

2. Generating Critical CSS

3. Implementation Considerations

Section 14.4: Lazy Loading CSS Resources

1. Understanding Lazy Loading CSS

2. Benefits of Lazy Loading CSS

2. Separate Concerns

3. Folder Structure

4. Modularize Component Styles

5. Use a Main Stylesheet

6. Minimize Global Scope

7. Use a Build Process

8. Version Control

Section 15.3: BEM (Block, Element, Modifier) Methodology

1. Understanding BEM

2. BEM Naming Convention

3. Benefits of BEM

4. BEM in Practice

5. Consistency is Key

Section 15.4: CSS Comments and Documentation

1. The Role of CSS Comments

2. Best Practices for CSS Comments

3. CSS Documentation Tools

Section 15.5: Version Control for CSS

1. The Importance of Version Control

2. Setting Up Version Control

3. Bold Typography

4. Gradient Backgrounds

5. Microinteractions

6. Illustrations and Custom Graphics

7. Responsive Typography

Section 17.2: Applying Design Trends with CSS

1. Implementing Responsive Design

2. Customizing Color Schemes

3. Typography Enhancements

4. Creating Engaging Microinteractions

5. Optimizing for Dark Mode

6. Utilizing Gradients

7. Incorporating Custom Graphics

Section 17.3: Responsive Typography and Color Schemes

Responsive Typography

Color Schemes

Section 17.4: Exploring Microinteractions

Understanding Microinteractions

Creating Microinteractions with CSS

Adding Microinteractions with JavaScript

Chapter 19: CSS Debugging and Troubleshooting

Section 19.1: Identifying and Fixing CSS Bugs

1. Replicate the Issue

2. Inspect Elements with Developer Tools

3. Check the CSS Rules

4. Check for Specificity Issues

5. Inspect Box Model Properties

6. Use Browser Compatibility Mode

7. Test Different Scenarios

8. Validate Your CSS

9. Seek Help and Documentation

10. Keep a Record

Section 19.2: Browser DevTools for CSS Debugging

Inspecting Elements

Viewing Applied Styles

Modifying Styles

Box Model Inspection

Pseudo-Element and Pseudo-Class Inspection

CSS Specificity and Inheritance

Color Picker

Chapter 20: Advanced CSS Techniques

Section 20.1: CSS Custom Properties (Variables)

What Are CSS Custom Properties?

Benefits of CSS Custom Properties

Using Custom Properties for Responsive Design

Browser Support

Conclusion

Section 20.2: CSS Houdini: Extending CSS's Capabilities

What is CSS Houdini?

Benefits of CSS Houdini

Browser Support

Getting Started with CSS Houdini

Conclusion

Section 20.3: CSS-in-JS: Styling with JavaScript

What is CSS-in-JS?

Popular CSS-in-JS Libraries

Benefits of CSS-in-JS

Challenges of CSS-in-JS

Conclusion

Chapter 1: Understanding CSS Fundamentals

Section 1.1: Introduction to CSS

Cascading Style Sheets (CSS) is a fundamental technology used in web development to control the presentation and layout of web pages. CSS allows you to define how HTML elements should appear on the screen, making it an essential tool for creating visually appealing and user-friendly websites.

What is CSS?

CSS is a stylesheet language that separates the content (HTML) from the presentation (CSS). It provides a way to define styles, such as colors, fonts, spacing, and layout, for HTML elements. This separation of concerns makes web development more efficient and maintainable.

CSS Syntax

CSS uses a simple syntax with properties and values. A CSS rule consists of a selector and a set of declarations enclosed in curly braces. Here's a basic example:

h1 {

color: blue;

font-size: 24px;

}

In this example, the selector h1 selects all <h1> elements, and the declarations inside the curly braces specify that the text color should be blue, and the font size should be 24 pixels.

Cascading and Specificity

The "C" in CSS stands for "Cascading," which refers to how styles are applied to elements. CSS rules can come from various sources, including external stylesheets, internal styles (within an HTML document), and inline styles. When multiple conflicting styles target the same element, the concept of specificity determines which style is applied.

CSS Selectors

CSS selectors are patterns used to select and style HTML elements. They can be based on element names, class names, IDs, attributes, and more. Here are some common selectors:

- Type selector: Selects elements by their HTML tag name (e.g., p selects all <p> elements).

- Class selector: Selects elements by their class attribute (e.g., .highlight selects elements with the highlight class).

- ID selector: Selects a specific element by its ID attribute (e.g., #header selects the element with id="header").

Linking CSS to HTML

To apply CSS styles to an HTML document, you need to link the CSS file to the HTML using the <link> element in the document's <head> section. Here's an example:

<!DOCTYPE html>

```
<html>

<head>

<link rel="stylesheet" type="text/css" href="styles.css">

</head>

<body>

<h1>Welcome to My Website</h1>

<p>This is a paragraph of text.</p>

</body>

</html>
```

In this example, the href attribute of the <link> element specifies the path to the CSS file (styles.css).

Inheritance

One of the powerful features of CSS is inheritance. When you apply a style to a parent element, its children can inherit those styles unless explicitly overridden. This helps maintain consistency throughout a website.

Summary

In this section, you've been introduced to CSS as a technology that separates the presentation of web pages from their content. You've learned about CSS syntax, selectors, cascading, specificity, and how to link CSS to HTML documents. CSS is a fundamental tool in web development, and understanding its basics is essential for building modern and responsive websites.

Section 1.2: CSS Selectors and Properties

CSS selectors and properties are the building blocks of styling web content. In this section, we'll dive deeper into the world of CSS selectors and explore some common CSS properties used for styling HTML elements.

CSS Selectors

CSS selectors determine which HTML elements will be targeted and styled. There are various types of selectors:

- **Type Selector**: This selects elements by their HTML tag name. For example, p selects all \<p\> elements on the page.

- **Class Selector**: It selects elements by their class attribute. For instance, .highlight targets all elements with the highlight class.

- **ID Selector**: This selects a specific element by its ID attribute. For example, #header targets the element with id="header".

- **Descendant Selector**: It selects elements that are descendants of a specified element. For instance, ul li selects all \<li\> elements inside a \<ul\>.

- **Child Selector**: This selects elements that are direct children of a specified element. For example, ul > li targets all \<li\> elements that are immediate children of a \<ul\>.

- **Pseudo-classes**: These are used to select elements based on their state or position. Common pseudo-classes include :hover for hover effects and :first-child to select the first child of an element.

CSS Properties

CSS properties define how selected elements should be styled. Some essential CSS properties include:

- **color**: Specifies the text color (e.g., color: red;).

- **font-size**: Sets the size of the font (e.g., font-size: 16px;).

- **background-color**: Defines the background color (e.g., background-color: #f0f0f0;).

- **margin**: Controls the outer spacing of an element (e.g., margin: 10px;).

- **padding**: Sets the inner spacing of an element (e.g., padding: 5px;).

- **border**: Defines the border around an element (e.g., border: 1px solid #000;).

- **width** and **height**: Specify the dimensions of an element (e.g., width: 200px; height: 100px;).

- **text-align**: Aligns the text within an element (e.g., text-align: center;).

- **font-family**: Sets the font family for text (e.g., font-family: Arial, sans-serif;).

Combining Selectors

CSS allows you to combine multiple selectors to target specific elements more precisely. For example, h1.title selects <h1> elements with the class title, and div.container p targets <p> elements within a <div> with the class container.

Grouping Selectors

You can group selectors together to apply the same styles to multiple elements. Separate selectors with commas to group them. For example:

h1, h2, h3 {

font-family: 'Helvetica', sans-serif;

color: #333;

}

In this example, the font family and text color are applied to <h1>, <h2>, and <h3> elements.

Inheritance of Properties

Some CSS properties are inherited by child elements from their parent. For example, if you set the font size on a parent element, its child elements will inherit that size unless overridden.

CSS Comments

Comments in CSS are enclosed in /* */. They are useful for adding explanations or notes to your CSS code without affecting the styling. For example:

/* *This is a comment* */

```
p {
```

font-size: 16px;

```
}
```

In summary, CSS selectors and properties are essential for styling web pages. Understanding how to select elements and apply styles using CSS is crucial for creating visually appealing and well-structured websites.

Section 1.3: Working with CSS Classes and IDs

In CSS, classes and IDs are valuable tools for applying styles to specific elements on a web page. They offer a way to target and style elements that may not be styled by their HTML tag or structure alone. In this section, we will explore how to use classes and IDs effectively in CSS.

CSS Classes

A CSS class is a reusable identifier that can be applied to one or more HTML elements. Classes are defined in your CSS stylesheets and can be assigned to elements in your HTML. To define a class in CSS, use a period (.) followed by the class name, like this:

.my-class {

/ CSS rules for .my-class go here */*

}

In your HTML, you can apply the class to an element like this:

<div class="my-class">

```
<!—Content goes here—>

</div>
```

By using classes, you can apply the same style to multiple elements across your website. It promotes consistency and simplifies maintenance.

CSS IDs

An ID is a unique identifier for an HTML element. Unlike classes, IDs must be unique within a single HTML document. To define an ID in CSS, use a hash (#) followed by the ID name, like this:

```
#my-id {

/* CSS rules for #my-id go here */

}
```

In your HTML, you can assign an ID to an element like this:

```
<div id="my-id">

<!—Content goes here—>

</div>
```

IDs are typically used for styling individual, unique elements on a page, such as a header or a specific section.

Specificity and CSS Classes/IDs

When it comes to specificity, IDs have higher specificity than classes. This means that if a conflict arises between a class and an ID targeting the same element, the ID's styles will take precedence. It's important to use this knowledge carefully to avoid unintended style overrides.

Multiple Classes

HTML elements can have multiple classes. To apply multiple classes to an element, separate them with spaces:

<div class="class1 class2">

<!—Content goes here—>

</div>

In this example, the element has both class1 and class2 applied, allowing you to combine styles from different classes.

Combining Classes and IDs

You can also combine classes and IDs to target elements with precision. For instance, if you have an element with both a class and an ID, you can target it like this:

#my-id.my-class {

/* CSS rules for #my-id with class .my-class go here */

}

This selector will select elements with both the ID my-id and the class my-class.

Best Practices

When working with classes and IDs in CSS, it's essential to follow best practices:

- Use classes for styling elements that share common styles across different parts of your website.

- Use IDs for styling unique elements that are not repeated on the same page.

- Avoid overusing IDs as they have higher specificity and can lead to style conflicts.

- Keep class and ID names descriptive and meaningful to make your code more maintainable.

- Use multiple classes to combine styles from different sources.

In summary, CSS classes and IDs are crucial for targeting and styling specific elements in your web page. By understanding their differences and best practices, you can effectively manage the styling of your web content.

Section 1.4: The Box Model: Margin, Border, and Padding

In CSS, the box model is a fundamental concept that defines how elements are displayed on a web page. Every HTML element is considered a rectangular box, and the box model describes the properties that affect its dimensions and spacing. This section explores the box model, including margin, border, and padding.

The Box Model Components

The box model consists of four main components:

1. **Content**: This is the innermost part of the box and

contains the actual content, such as text, images, or other elements.

2. **Padding**: Padding is the space between the content and the element's border. You can control the padding using CSS properties like padding-top, padding-right, padding-bottom, and padding-left.

3. **Border**: The border is a line that surrounds the content and padding. You can specify the border's width, style, and color using CSS properties like border-width, border-style, and border-color.

4. **Margin**: The margin is the space outside the element's border. It creates separation between elements. You can control the margin using CSS properties like margin-top, margin-right, margin-bottom, and margin-left.

Box Model Diagram

Here's a visual representation of the box model:

————————-

| Margin |

| |

| ————— |

| | Border | |

| | | |

| | Content | |

| | | |

| ————— |

| |

| Margin |

————————-

Box Sizing

By default, the total width and height of an element include the content, padding, and border, but not the margin. This is known as the "content-box" value for the box-sizing property. You can change this behavior to include padding and border in the element's dimensions by using the "border-box" value for box-sizing. This can be helpful for simplifying layout calculations.

```
/* Example of box-sizing property */

.box {

box-sizing: border-box;

width: 200px; /* This width includes padding and border */

padding: 20px;

border: 5px solid #333;

margin: 10px;

}
```

Margin Collapse

Margin collapse is a behavior in CSS where the margins of adjacent elements can collapse into a single margin. It occurs in certain situations, such as when top and bottom margins of sibling elements touch. Understanding margin collapse is important when working with layout design.

Practical Use of the Box Model

The box model is foundational for web layout and design. By controlling the padding, border, and margin of elements, you can create visually appealing and well-structured web pages. It's essential to have a good grasp of the box model when working with CSS layout frameworks like Flexbox and CSS Grid.

In summary, the box model is a core concept in CSS that governs how elements are displayed on a web page. Understanding how the content, padding, border, and margin interact is crucial for effective web design and layout.

Section 1.5: CSS Layout and Positioning

CSS layout and positioning are essential aspects of web design. They allow you to control the arrangement and positioning of elements on a web page, creating the desired structure and visual hierarchy. In this section, we'll explore CSS layout techniques and positioning properties.

CSS Display Property

The display property in CSS determines how an element should be displayed. Common values for the display property include:

- block: Elements with this value create a block-level box that spans the entire width of their parent container. Block elements stack vertically by default.

• inline: Elements with this value create an inline-level box that flows with the surrounding content. Inline elements stack horizontally by default.

• inline-block: Combines features of both block and inline elements, allowing you to control the dimensions and layout of elements while keeping them inline within the content flow.

• none: Elements with this value are not displayed on the page and occupy no space. This is often used for hiding elements dynamically with JavaScript.

CSS Position Property

The position property in CSS is used to control the positioning of elements. It has several values, including:

• static (default): Elements with position: static are positioned according to the normal flow of the document. Top, bottom, left, and right properties have no effect.

• relative: Elements with position: relative are positioned relative to their normal position in the document flow. You can use top, right, bottom, and left properties to offset them from their original position.

• absolute: Elements with position: absolute are positioned relative to their nearest positioned ancestor. If no positioned ancestor exists, they are positioned relative to the initial containing block (usually the <html> element).

- fixed: Elements with position: fixed are positioned relative to the viewport and do not move when the page is scrolled. They are often used for creating elements like fixed navigation bars.

CSS Float Property

The float property is used for text wrapping and layout. When an element is floated, it is taken out of the normal document flow and moved to the left or right until it reaches the edge of its containing element or another floated element. This is commonly used for creating multi-column layouts.

/* Example of using float */

.float-left {

float: left;

width: 50%;

}

.float-right {

float: right;

width: 50%;

}

CSS Clear Property

The clear property is often used in conjunction with floated elements to control their positioning and prevent unwanted overlaps. It specifies whether an element should be positioned below, above, or beside the floated elements within the same container.

```
/* Example of using clear */

.clearfix::after {

content: "";

display: table;

clear: both;

}
```

CSS Flexbox and Grid

Modern CSS layout techniques, such as Flexbox and Grid, have revolutionized web design by providing powerful tools for creating complex layouts with ease. Flexbox is ideal for one-dimensional layouts, while Grid is suited for two-dimensional layouts.

Flexbox allows you to create flexible and responsive designs by aligning elements along a single axis (either horizontally or vertically). It's particularly useful for building navigation menus, lists, and card layouts.

Grid, on the other hand, allows you to create grid-based layouts with rows and columns. It provides precise control over the placement and alignment of elements within the grid, making it suitable for creating complex web applications with intricate layouts.

```
/* Example of using Flexbox */

.container {

display: flex;

justify-content: center; /* Horizontal centering */
```

align-items: center; /* *Vertical centering* */

}

/* *Example of using Grid* */

.grid-container {

display: grid;

grid-template-columns: repeat(3, 1fr); /* *Three equal-width columns* */

grid-gap: 20px; /* *Spacing between grid items* */

}

CSS Positioning and Z-Index

When working with layered elements, the z-index property allows you to control the stacking order of elements on the z-axis. Elements with higher z-index values appear on top of elements with lower values. This is particularly useful for creating overlays, tooltips, and dropdown menus.

/* *Example of using z-index* */

.overlay {

position: fixed;

top: 0;

left: 0;

width: 100%;

height: 100%;

background-color: rgba(0, 0, 0, 0.5);

z-index: 999; /* *Higher z-index for overlay* */

}

.tooltip {

position: absolute;

background-color: #333;

color: #fff;

padding: 5px;

z-index: 1000; /* *Higher z-index for tooltip* */

}

In summary, CSS layout and positioning are fundamental to web design. Understanding how to use the display, position, float, and other layout properties enables you to create responsive and visually appealing web pages. Additionally, modern layout techniques like Flexbox and Grid provide powerful tools for building complex layouts with ease.

Chapter 2: Mastering CSS Selectors

Section 2.1: Basic Selectors: Type, Class, ID

CSS selectors are instrumental in targeting HTML elements for styling. In this section, we'll delve into the fundamentals of CSS selectors, including type selectors, class selectors, and ID selectors.

Type Selectors

Type selectors, also known as element selectors, are the most basic form of selectors. They target HTML elements based on their tag name. For example, to style all <p> elements on a page, you would use a type selector:

p {

/* CSS rules for all <p> elements */

}

Type selectors are useful for applying consistent styles to all instances of a specific HTML element. However, they lack specificity, which means they can affect all instances of the element type on the page.

Class Selectors

Class selectors allow you to target elements based on their class attribute. Classes are defined in HTML using the class attribute and are preceded by a period (dot) in CSS. For example, to style elements with the class "highlight," you would use a class selector:

.highlight {

/* CSS rules for elements with class "highlight" */

}

Class selectors are versatile and can be applied to multiple elements on a page. They are particularly valuable for styling groups of elements with shared characteristics.

ID Selectors

ID selectors target elements with a specific ID attribute. In HTML, the ID is defined using the id attribute, and in CSS, it is preceded by a hash (#) symbol. ID selectors are unique on a page, and they have higher specificity compared to type and class selectors. Here's an example:

```html
<div id="header">

<!—Content goes here—>

</div>
```

```css
#header {

/* CSS rules for the element with ID "header" */

}
```

ID selectors are typically used for styling individual, unique elements. However, it's crucial to use them sparingly because overusing IDs can lead to specificity issues and make the CSS harder to maintain.

Combining Selectors

Selectors can be combined to target elements more precisely. For example, you can use a type selector with a class selector to style specific elements:

h1.title {

/ CSS rules for <h1> elements with class "title" */*

}

This selector targets <h1> elements that also have the "title" class.

Specificity and Order of Application

When multiple selectors target the same element, CSS specificity determines which styles take precedence. The order in which the styles are defined also matters. Styles defined later in the CSS file override styles defined earlier, assuming equal specificity.

In summary, CSS selectors are essential for applying styles to HTML elements. Type selectors target elements by tag name, class selectors target elements by class attribute, and ID selectors target elements by ID attribute. Understanding selector specificity and the order of style application is crucial for effective CSS styling.

Section 2.2: Combining Selectors: Grouping and Nesting

In CSS, it's often necessary to target multiple elements at once or apply styles to elements within specific contexts. Section 2.2 covers combining selectors through grouping and nesting, enabling you to create complex and fine-grained styling rules for your web page.

Grouping Selectors

CSS allows you to group multiple selectors together to apply the same styles to multiple elements. To group selectors, separate them with commas. For example:

```
h1, h2, h3 {

font-family: 'Arial', sans-serif;

color: #333;

}
```

In this example, styles for font family and text color are applied to <h1>, <h2>, and <h3> elements. Grouping selectors can help reduce redundancy in your CSS code.

Descendant Selectors

Descendant selectors, also known as contextual selectors, allow you to target elements that are descendants of another element. This is useful for styling elements within a specific context, such as a navigation menu within a header.

```
.header ul {

/* CSS rules for <ul> elements inside elements with class "header" */

}
```

In this example, the style applies to all <ul> elements that are descendants of elements with the class "header." This selector targets only the relevant <ul> elements without affecting other lists on the page.

Child Selectors

Child selectors are similar to descendant selectors, but they only target elements that are direct children of another element. They use the greater-than sign (>) to specify the relationship.

```
nav > ul {
```

```
/* CSS rules for <ul> elements that are direct children of <nav> */

}
```

This selector targets <ul> elements that are immediate children of a <nav> element. It won't select <ul> elements that are deeper in the hierarchy.

Adjacent Sibling Selectors

Adjacent sibling selectors target elements that are immediately preceded by another element with the same parent. They use the plus sign (+) to specify the relationship.

```
h2 + p {

/* CSS rules for <p> elements that directly follow <h2> elements */

}
```

In this example, the styles are applied to <p> elements that immediately follow <h2> elements. It's a powerful way to style elements based on their position in the document.

General Sibling Selectors

General sibling selectors target elements that are siblings of another element with the same parent, regardless of their position. They use the tilde sign (~) to specify the relationship.

```
h2 ~ p {

/* CSS rules for <p> elements that are siblings of <h2> elements */

}
```

This selector targets all <p> elements that share the same parent as <h2> elements, regardless of their position in the document.

Pseudo-Classes and Pseudo-Elements

In addition to basic selectors, CSS provides pseudo-classes and pseudo-elements to style elements based on various conditions and parts of the element, such as its state or content. Examples include :hover for hover effects, :nth-child() for selecting elements by their position, and ::before and ::after for adding generated content.

```css
/* Example of using :hover pseudo-class */

button:hover {

background-color: #007bff;

color: #fff;

}

/* Example of using ::before pseudo-element */

p::before {

content: "Read this: ";

font-weight: bold;

}
```

These selectors and pseudo-elements add interactivity and customization to your web page styling.

In summary, combining selectors in CSS through grouping and nesting is a powerful way to target specific elements and create complex styling rules. Understanding how to use descendant, child, adjacent sibling, and general sibling selectors, along with pseudo-classes and pseudo-elements, provides you with fine-grained control over the appearance of your web page.

Section 2.3: Pseudo-Classes and Pseudo-Elements

Pseudo-classes and pseudo-elements are valuable tools in CSS for selecting and styling elements based on various conditions, states, or parts of an element. This section explores how to use them effectively in your CSS styling.

Pseudo-Classes

Pseudo-classes are used to select elements based on their state or specific conditions. They are preceded by a colon (:). Some commonly used pseudo-classes include:

- :hover: Selects an element when the mouse pointer hovers over it. This is often used for creating interactive hover effects on links and buttons.

- :active: Selects an element when it is being activated, such as when a user clicks on a link or button. It is useful for creating visual feedback during user interactions.

- :focus: Selects an element when it gains focus, typically through keyboard navigation or clicking. It is commonly used to style form elements like input fields.

- :nth-child(): Selects elements based on their position among siblings. You can specify a formula inside the parentheses to target specific elements in a group. For example, :nth-child(odd) selects all odd-numbered elements.

```
/* Example of using :hover and :active pseudo-classes */

a:hover {

text-decoration: underline;

}

button:active {

background-color: #ff5733;

}

/* Example of using :nth-child() pseudo-class */

li:nth-child(odd) {

background-color: #f2f2f2;

}
```

Pseudo-classes add interactivity and visual enhancements to your web page.

Pseudo-Elements

Pseudo-elements allow you to style specific parts of an element. They are preceded by a double colon (::). Commonly used pseudo-elements include:

- ::before: Inserts content before the content of an element. This is often used for adding decorative elements or labels before text.

- ::after: Inserts content after the content of an element. It is useful for adding icons, tooltips, or additional information.

- ::first-line: Styles the first line of text within an element. You can use it to apply unique styles to the first line of a paragraph or heading.

- ::first-letter: Styles the first letter of text within an element. It is often used for drop caps or decorative initial letters.

```
/* Example of using ::before and ::after pseudo-elements */

blockquote::before {

content: "\201C"; /* Opening double quotation mark */

font-size: 24px;

}

blockquote::after {

content: "\201D"; /* Closing double quotation mark */

font-size: 24px;

}

/* Example of using ::first-line and ::first-letter pseudo-elements */

p::first-line {

font-weight: bold;

}
```

```
p::first-letter {

font-size: 36px;

float: left;

margin-right: 10px;

}
```

Pseudo-elements allow you to create decorative and customized elements within your content.

Combining Pseudo-Classes and Pseudo-Elements

You can combine pseudo-classes and pseudo-elements to create complex and specific styling rules. For example, you can use ::before and :hover together to add additional content when an element is hovered over.

```
/* Example of combining ::before and :hover */

a::before {

content: "◈"; /* Unicode emoji for link icon */

margin-right: 5px;

opacity: 0;

transition: opacity 0.3s ease;

}

a:hover::before {

opacity: 1;

}
```

In this example, a link icon is displayed before the link text when the link is hovered over.

In summary, pseudo-classes and pseudo-elements in CSS provide a powerful way to select and style elements based on various conditions and specific parts of an element. Understanding their usage enhances your ability to create interactive and visually appealing web pages.

Section 2.4: Attribute Selectors and CSS3 Selectors

Attribute selectors in CSS allow you to target HTML elements based on the presence or values of their attributes. Additionally, CSS3 introduces advanced selectors that provide even more precise control over element selection. This section explores attribute selectors and some of the CSS3 selectors.

Attribute Selectors

Attribute selectors are used to select elements based on the attributes they possess. These selectors are enclosed in square brackets [...]. There are several ways to use attribute selectors:

- **Existence Attribute Selector**: It selects elements that have a specific attribute, regardless of its value.

/* Select all <a> elements with a "target" attribute */

a[target] {

text-decoration: underline;

}

- **Exact Attribute Value Selector**: It selects elements with a specific attribute value.

/* Select all <input> elements with a "type" attribute equal to "text" */

input[type="text"] {

border: 1px solid #ccc;

}

- **Partial Attribute Value Selector**: It selects elements with attributes containing a specified substring.

/* Select all elements with a "class" attribute containing "highlight" */

[class*="highlight"] {

background-color: yellow;

}

- **Starts with Attribute Value Selector**: It selects elements with attributes that start with a specified value.

/* Select all <a> elements with an "href" attribute starting with "https://" */

a[href^="https://"] {

color: #007bff;

}

- **Ends with Attribute Value Selector**: It selects elements with attributes that end with a specified value.

```
/* Select all <a> elements with an "href" attribute ending with ".pdf"
*/

a[href$=".pdf"] {

font-weight: bold;

}
```

Attribute selectors are powerful for targeting specific elements with precise criteria.

CSS3 Selectors

CSS3 introduces several advanced selectors that offer greater control over element selection. Some notable CSS3 selectors include:

- **:not() Selector**: It selects elements that do not match a given selector.

```
/* Select all <li> elements that are not the first child */

li:not(:first-child) {

margin-left: 10px;

}
```

- **:nth-child() and :nth-of-type() Selectors**: These selectors allow you to select elements based on their position among siblings.

```
/* Select every even <tr> element within a <table> */

tr:nth-child(even) {

background-color: #f2f2f2;
```

}

- **:checked Selector**: It selects input elements that are checked.

/* Style the label of checked checkboxes */

input[type="checkbox"]:**checked** + label {

font-weight: bold;

}

- **:focus-within Selector**: It selects an element if any of its descendants have focus.

/* Style the container when an input field inside it has focus */

.container:**focus-within** {

border: 2px solid #007bff;

}

These advanced selectors provide fine-grained control over element styling and interactions.

In summary, attribute selectors and CSS3 selectors expand your CSS toolkit by allowing you to select elements based on attributes, values, positions, and other criteria. Understanding and using these selectors can help you create more dynamic and tailored styles for your web pages.

Section 2.5: Advanced Selectors for Responsive Design

Responsive design is a crucial aspect of modern web development, ensuring that websites look and function well on various devices and screen sizes. In this section, we'll explore advanced CSS selectors that help you create responsive layouts and styles.

Media Queries

Media queries are the foundation of responsive web design. They allow you to apply different styles to elements based on the characteristics of the device, such as its screen width, height, or orientation. Media queries are defined using the @media rule.

```
/* Example of a media query */

@media screen and (max-width: 768px) {

/* Styles for screens with a maximum width of 768px */

body {

font-size: 16px;

}

}
```

In this example, the font size of the body element changes when the screen width is 768 pixels or less.

Viewport Units

Viewport units (vw, vh, vmin, and vmax) are relative units that allow you to size elements based on the viewport's dimensions (the visible area of the browser window). They are particularly useful for creating fluid and responsive layouts.

- vw: 1% of the viewport's width.

- vh: 1% of the viewport's height.

- vmin: 1% of the smaller dimension (width or height) of the viewport.

- vmax: 1% of the larger dimension (width or height) of the viewport.

/* Example of using viewport units for responsive typography */

h1 {

font-size: 4vw; /* Font size is 4% of the viewport's width */

}

Flexbox and Grid for Responsive Layouts

Flexbox and CSS Grid are powerful layout tools for creating responsive designs. They allow you to build complex layouts that adapt to different screen sizes and orientations.

Flexbox is well-suited for one-dimensional layouts, such as navigation menus or lists, where elements flow in a row or column. It provides properties like flex-direction and justify-content to control layout.

/* Example of using Flexbox for responsive navigation */

.nav {

display: flex;

```css
flex-direction: column; /* Vertical layout on small screens */

}

.nav-item {

margin-bottom: 10px;

}

@media screen and (min-width: 768px) {

.nav {

flex-direction: row; /* Horizontal layout on larger screens */

justify-content: space-between; /* Distribute items evenly */

}

}
```

CSS Grid is ideal for two-dimensional layouts, such as grid-based galleries or complex forms. It offers properties like grid-template-columns and grid-gap to create grid structures.

```css
/* Example of using CSS Grid for responsive grid layout */

.grid-container {

display: grid;

grid-template-columns: 1fr; /* Single column on small screens */

grid-gap: 10px;

}

@media screen and (min-width: 768px) {
```

```
.grid-container {

grid-template-columns: repeat(2, 1fr); /* Two columns on larger
screens */

}

}
```

Advanced Attribute Selectors for Responsive Images

Attribute selectors can be used for responsive images. For instance, you can select images with specific file formats (e.g., JPEG or PNG) or alt text for accessibility.

```
/* Select images with JPEG format */

img[src$=".jpg"] {

max-width: 100%;

height: auto;

}

/* Select images with specific alt text */

img[alt="Logo"] {

border: 2px solid #007bff;

}
```

These selectors help you optimize images for different devices and improve accessibility.

Custom Properties (CSS Variables)

Custom properties, also known as CSS variables, enable you to define reusable values in your CSS and change them dynamically with media queries. This flexibility is valuable for responsive design.

```
/* Define a custom property */

:root {

—primary-color: #007bff;

}
/* Use the custom property */

.button {

background-color: var(—primary-color);

}
/* Change the custom property value for different screen sizes */

@media screen and (max-width: 768px) {

:root {

—primary-color: #ff5733;

}

}
```

Custom properties make it easy to update colors, sizes, and other values across your website for different device conditions.

In summary, responsive design is essential for ensuring that your web content adapts to various screen sizes and devices. Advanced CSS selectors, media queries, viewport units, layout tools like Flexbox and Grid, and CSS variables play a significant role in creating responsive and user-friendly web experiences.

Chapter 3: Styling Text and Fonts

Section 3.1: Changing Font Family and Size

In web design, typography plays a crucial role in conveying information effectively and enhancing the visual appeal of a website. CSS provides extensive capabilities for styling text and fonts, allowing you to control aspects such as font family, size, color, and spacing. In this section, we'll focus on changing font family and size, two fundamental aspects of text styling.

Font Family

The font-family property in CSS enables you to specify the typeface or font family for text elements. Font families are typically categorized into two groups: generic fonts and specific fonts.

Generic Fonts

Generic fonts are broad categories of fonts that provide a fallback option in case the specified font is not available on the user's device. Common generic font families include:

- serif: This category includes fonts with serifs, which are small decorative lines at the ends of characters. Serif fonts are often associated with a formal and traditional look.

- sans-serif: Sans-serif fonts do not have serifs and are known for their clean and modern appearance. They are commonly used for digital content.

- monospace: Monospace fonts have fixed-width characters, where each character takes up the same amount of horizontal space. They are often used for code and programming.

- cursive: Cursive fonts mimic handwritten text and provide a decorative and artistic style.

- fantasy: Fantasy fonts are less common and often used for special effects or creative designs.

Here's an example of how to use the font-family property with generic font families:

/* Applying a generic font family */

body {

font-family: Arial, sans-serif; /* *Arial if available, sans-serif as a fallback* */

}

Specific Fonts

Specific fonts are custom fonts that you can include in your website using web font services like Google Fonts or by specifying font files hosted on your server. To use a specific font, you need to provide the font's name or URL in the font-family property.

/* Using a specific font from Google Fonts */

body {

font-family: 'Open Sans', sans-serif; /* *Open Sans if available, sans-serif as a fallback* */

}

Font Size

The font-size property controls the size of text. You can specify the size in various units, including pixels (px), ems (em), rems (rem), percentages (%), and more.

/* Setting font size in pixels */

h1 {

font-size: 24px;

}

/* Setting font size in ems */

p {

font-size: 1.2em; /* 1.2 times the font size of the parent element */

}

It's important to choose an appropriate font size to ensure readability and a harmonious overall design. Responsive web design often involves using relative units like ems or rems to adapt text size to different screen sizes.

Font Weight and Style

In addition to font family and size, you can control other text properties such as font weight (boldness) and style (italicization):

/* Setting font weight to bold */

strong {

font-weight: bold;

```
}
```

/ Setting font style to italic */*

```
em {
```

font-style: italic;

```
}
```

These properties give you fine-grained control over how text elements appear on your web page.

In summary, changing font family and size are fundamental aspects of text styling in CSS. You can choose between generic and specific font families, specify font sizes in various units, and control font weight and style to create visually appealing and readable text on your website. Typography plays a significant role in the overall design and user experience of a web page, making it an important skill for web developers and designers.

Section 3.2: Text Color and Typography

Text color and typography are essential aspects of web design that greatly influence the readability and visual appeal of your website. In this section, we'll explore how to control text color and typography using CSS.

Text Color

The color property in CSS allows you to specify the color of text elements. You can use various color notations, including named colors, hexadecimal values, RGB, RGBA, HSL, and HSLA.

/ Setting text color using named color */*

```css
p {
color: red;
}
/* Setting text color using hexadecimal value */
h1 {
color: #007bff; /* A shade of blue */
}
/* Setting text color using RGB */
a {
color: rgb(255, 0, 0); /* Red */
}
/* Setting text color using RGBA with transparency */
button {
color: rgba(0, 128, 0, 0.8); /* Semi-transparent green */
}
/* Setting text color using HSL */
span {
color: hsl(210, 100%, 50%); /* Pure green */
}
```

Choosing an appropriate text color is crucial for readability and ensuring that text contrasts well with the background color or image.

Accessibility guidelines also recommend a sufficient contrast ratio between text and its background to make content accessible to all users.

Font Style and Weight

In addition to font size, you can control font style and weight to enhance typography.

Font Style

The font-style property allows you to set the style of text as normal, italic, or oblique. Italic text is often used to emphasize words or phrases.

```
/* Setting font style to italic */

em {

font-style: italic;

}
```

Font Weight

The font-weight property defines the thickness or boldness of text. You can specify values like normal, bold, or numeric values ranging from 100 (thin) to 900 (extra bold).

```
/* Setting font weight to bold */

strong {

font-weight: bold;

}
```

Line Height and Letter Spacing

Proper line height (line-height) and letter spacing (letter-spacing) are essential for improving readability and aesthetics. Line height determines the vertical space between lines of text, while letter spacing adjusts the space between individual characters.

```
/* Setting line height and letter spacing */

p {

line-height: 1.5; /* 1.5 times the font size */

letter-spacing: 1px;

}
```

Applying appropriate line height and letter spacing can prevent text from appearing too cramped or too spread out.

Text Transform

The text-transform property allows you to control the capitalization of text. It can be used to convert text to uppercase, lowercase, or capitalize the first letter of each word.

```
/* Transform text to uppercase */

h2 {

text-transform: uppercase;

}

/* Transform text to capitalize the first letter of each word */

blockquote {
```

text-transform: capitalize;

}

This property is handy for maintaining consistent text styling.

Text Decoration

Text decoration properties (text-decoration, text-decoration-line, text-decoration-style, and text-decoration-color) enable you to add visual effects to text, such as underlines, overlines, and strikethroughs.

/* Adding an underline to links */

a {

text-decoration: underline;

}

/* Adding a wavy underline with a custom color */

button {

text-decoration-line: underline;

text-decoration-style: wavy;

text-decoration-color: #007bff;

}

Text decoration is often used for links, buttons, and other interactive elements.

In summary, controlling text color and typography is essential for creating visually appealing and readable web content. CSS provides a wide range of properties to adjust text color, style, weight, line height, letter spacing, capitalization, and text decoration. Careful selection and styling of text elements can significantly enhance the design and user experience of your website.

Section 3.3: Text Decoration and Spacing

Text decoration and spacing are essential aspects of text styling in web design. They allow you to enhance the visual appearance and readability of your text content. In this section, we'll delve into text decoration options and techniques for adjusting spacing between characters and words.

Text Decoration

Text decoration refers to visual effects applied to text, such as underlines, overlines, and strikethroughs. CSS provides several properties to control text decoration:

- text-decoration-line: Specifies the type of decoration, including values like underline, overline, line-through, none, or a combination of these.

```css
/* Adding an underline to links */

a {

text-decoration-line: underline;

}

/* Adding an overline and strikethrough to emphasized text */

em {

text-decoration-line: overline line-through;
```

}

- text-decoration-color: Sets the color of the decoration. You can use color values, including named colors, hexadecimal, RGB, or HSL.

/* Customizing the color of the underline */

a {

text-decoration-line: underline;

text-decoration-color: #007bff; /* Blue color */

}

- text-decoration-style: Determines the style of the decoration, such as solid, double, dotted, wavy, or initial.

/* Applying a wavy underline to links */

a {

text-decoration-line: underline;

text-decoration-style: wavy;

}

These text decoration properties allow you to create visually engaging links, emphasize text, or indicate content changes.

Letter Spacing

Letter spacing, controlled by the letter-spacing property, adjusts the space between individual characters in text. It is often used to improve readability or create specific design effects.

```css
/* Increasing letter spacing for a title */

h1 {

letter-spacing: 2px;

}

/* Reducing letter spacing for a blockquote */

blockquote {

letter-spacing: -0.5px; /* Negative value for tighter spacing */

}
```

Letter spacing can be customized to achieve the desired typographic effect. Negative values can be used for tighter character spacing, while positive values increase spacing.

Word Spacing

Word spacing, controlled by the word-spacing property, adjusts the space between words in a block of text. Like letter spacing, it can enhance readability and aesthetics.

```css
/* Increasing word spacing for a paragraph */

p {

word-spacing: 3px;

}

/* Reducing word spacing for a caption */

figcaption {

word-spacing: -1px; /* Negative value for tighter spacing */
```

}

Appropriate word spacing helps prevent text from appearing too cramped or too spread out, improving overall text presentation.

Text Transform

While not directly related to text decoration or spacing, the text-transform property can influence text appearance by controlling capitalization. It offers values like uppercase, lowercase, capitalize, and none.

/* Transform text to uppercase for navigation links */

nav a {

text-transform: uppercase;

}

/* Capitalize the first letter of each word in article titles */

article h2 {

text-transform: capitalize;

}

text-transform is useful for maintaining consistent text styling and emphasizing specific text elements.

In summary, text decoration and spacing are essential tools for text styling in web design. You can use text decoration properties to add underlines, overlines, and strikethroughs to text, while letter spacing and word spacing properties enable you to adjust the space between characters and words. These techniques enhance the visual appeal and readability of your web content, contributing to a more engaging user experience.

Section 3.4: Web Fonts and Icon Fonts

Web fonts are a powerful tool in web design that allow you to use custom typefaces and fonts in your web projects. They enable you to go beyond the limited set of fonts available on users' devices and create unique typography that matches your design vision. In this section, we'll explore web fonts and their integration into web pages. Additionally, we'll briefly touch on icon fonts, which are a specialized use case of web fonts for displaying icons.

Web Fonts

Web fonts, also known as custom fonts or downloadable fonts, are font files that are hosted on a web server and loaded into a web page to be displayed to visitors. They come in various formats, including TrueType Fonts (TTF), OpenType Fonts (OTF), Web Open Font Format (WOFF), and Web Open Font Format 2 (WOFF2). Here's how you can use web fonts in your CSS to apply custom typography to your web content:

1. **Font Hosting**: First, you need to host the font files on a server or use a font service like Google Fonts or Adobe Fonts. These services provide a wide selection of free and premium fonts that you can use in your projects.
2. **Linking the Font**: To use a web font, you typically link to it in your HTML document's <head> section. Here's an example of linking to a font from Google Fonts:

<link

href="https://fonts.googleapis.com/
css2?family=Roboto:wght@400;700&display=swap"

rel="stylesheet"

/>

1. **Applying the Font**: Once the font is linked, you can use it in your CSS by specifying the font-family property:

body {

font-family: 'Roboto', sans-serif;

}

In this example, we're using the 'Roboto' font, and if it's not available, we fall back to a generic sans-serif font.

1. **Font Variation**: Some web fonts provide variations such as different weights (e.g., regular and bold) or styles (e.g., italic). You can apply these variations using the font-weight and font-style properties:

h1 {

font-family: 'Roboto', sans-serif;

font-weight: 700; /* *Bold* */

font-style: italic;

}

Web fonts offer a wide range of design possibilities, allowing you to match your typography with your brand identity or design theme.

Icon Fonts

Icon fonts are a specialized type of web font that consists of symbols and icons instead of traditional characters. They are widely used for displaying scalable vector icons on web pages. Icon fonts are a convenient way to add icons to your website without using image files. Here's how you can use icon fonts:

1. **Select an Icon Font**: Choose an icon font library such as Font Awesome, Material Icons, or Ionicons. These libraries provide a collection of icons along with CSS classes for easy integration.
2. **Include the Icon Font**: Similar to web fonts, you include the icon font's CSS file in your HTML document:

<link

rel="stylesheet"

href="https://cdnjs.cloudflare.com/ajax/libs/font-awesome/6.0.0-beta3/css/all.min.css"

/>

1. **Use Icon Classes**: To display an icon, add a specific class to an HTML element. For example, to display a Facebook icon:

<i class="fab fa-facebook"></i>

The fab class indicates that it's a brand icon (Font Awesome's convention), and fa-facebook specifies the Facebook icon.

1. **Styling Icons**: You can style icon fonts just like any other text content using CSS. For example, you can change their color, size, or add animations.

.fab.fa-facebook {

color: #1877f2; /* *Facebook blue* */

font-size: 24px;

}

This CSS rule changes the color and size of the Facebook icon.

Icon fonts are popular for creating interactive and visually appealing user interfaces. They are also responsive and scale well to different screen sizes.

In summary, web fonts and icon fonts are valuable resources for enhancing typography and adding icons to web pages. Web fonts allow you to use custom typefaces, while icon fonts simplify the inclusion of scalable vector icons in your designs. When used effectively, they contribute to a polished and visually appealing web experience.

Section 3.5: Customizing Lists and Counters

Lists are a common element in web content, used for presenting information in an organized and structured manner. CSS provides powerful tools for customizing the appearance of lists and their associated counters (such as numbers or bullets). In this section, we'll explore how to style lists and counters to match your design preferences.

Styling Bulleted Lists

Bulleted lists are often used for presenting items without a specific order. By default, browsers apply a standard bullet point style. However, you can customize the appearance of these bullets using CSS. Here's how:

```
/* Changing the bullet style to a filled circle */

ul {

list-style-type: disc;

}

/* Using a custom image as the bullet */

ul.custom-bullet {

list-style-image: url('bullet.png');

}

/* Removing bullets from a list */

ul.no-bullet {

list-style-type: none;

}
```

In the first example, we change the bullet style to a filled circle using the list-style-type property. In the second example, we use a custom image as the bullet point by specifying a URL with list-style-image. Finally, in the third example, we remove the bullets altogether using list-style-type: none.

Styling Numbered Lists

Numbered lists, often used for ordered steps or instructions, can also be customized with CSS. You can change the numbering style or format, or even use custom content for list item counters.

```css
/* Changing the numbering style to Roman numerals */

ol.roman {

list-style-type: upper-roman;

}

/* Using custom content for list item counters */

ol.custom-counter {

list-style-type: none;

}

ol.custom-counter li::before {

content: 'Step ';

counter-increment: step-counter;

}

/* Restarting the numbering at a specific value */

ol.restart {

list-style-type: decimal;

}

ol.restart {
```

counter-reset: item-counter 5; /* *Restart numbering at 5* */

}

In the first example, we change the numbering style to upper-case Roman numerals. In the second example, we remove the default numbering and create custom content for list item counters using the ::before pseudo-element. In the third example, we restart the numbering at a specific value using counter-reset.

Nested Lists and Counters

Nested lists present a challenge when styling because they can inherit the styles of their parent lists. To maintain consistency, you can use the list-style shorthand property to set both the type and position of list markers:

/* *Customizing nested list markers* */

ul.nested {

list-style: square inside;

}

ol.nested {

list-style: decimal outside;

}

In this example, we specify the marker type as squares for unordered nested lists and decimal numbers for ordered nested lists. The inside and outside values determine whether the markers are placed inside or outside the list item box.

Styling List Item Content

You can also apply styles directly to the content of list items, such as text color, font size, or background color. This allows you to create visually appealing list items:

```css
/* Styling list item content */

li {

color: #333;

font-size: 16px;

background-color: #f8f8f8;

padding: 5px;

}
```

In this example, we set the text color, font size, background color, and padding for list items.

In summary, CSS offers extensive customization options for lists and counters, allowing you to tailor their appearance to match your website's design. Whether you're working with bulleted lists, numbered lists, nested lists, or list item content, CSS provides the flexibility to create visually appealing and organized content structures.

Chapter 4: Working with Colors and Backgrounds

Section 4.1: Color Values and Transparency

Colors are a fundamental aspect of web design, allowing you to create visually appealing and engaging websites. In CSS, you can specify colors using various notations and formats, and you can also apply transparency to colors for special effects. In this section, we'll explore different color value formats and techniques for working with transparency in CSS.

Color Notations

CSS supports several color notations to define colors:

1. **Named Colors**: CSS provides a set of named colors such as "red," "blue," "green," and many more. These are easy to use and remember.

/* Using named colors */

h1 {

color: red;

}

1. **Hexadecimal Notation**: Hexadecimal notation represents colors using a combination of six or three hexadecimal digits, specifying the amount of red, green, and blue (RGB) components.

/* Using hexadecimal notation */

```
p {

color: #00ff00; /* Green */

}
```

1. **RGB and RGBA**: RGB notation allows you to define colors using the red, green, and blue component values, each ranging from 0 to 255. RGBA is an extension of RGB that includes an alpha channel for transparency control.

```
/* Using RGB and RGBA */

span {

color: rgb(255, 0, 0); /* Red */

background-color:    rgba(0,    0,    255,    0.5);    /*
Semi-transparent blue */

}
```

1. **HSL and HSLA**: HSL notation defines colors using hue, saturation, and lightness values. HSLA includes an alpha channel for transparency.

```
/* Using HSL and HSLA */

a {

color: hsl(120, 100%, 50%); /* Green */

background-color:    hsla(240,    100%,    50%,    0.7);    /*
Semi-transparent blue */

}
```

1. **Keyword Values:** CSS includes some keyword values like "transparent" and "currentColor" for specific color effects.

    /* Using keyword values */

    button {

    background-color: transparent;

    }

Transparency with RGBA and HSLA

RGBA and HSLA notations allow you to control the transparency of colors by specifying an alpha value between 0 (completely transparent) and 1 (fully opaque). This feature is useful for creating overlays, gradients, or backgrounds with varying levels of transparency.

/* Creating a semi-transparent background */

.header {

background-color: rgba(0, 0, 0, 0.7); /* Black with 70% transparency */

}

/* Applying a partially transparent text shadow */

blockquote {

text-shadow: 2px 2px 4px rgba(0, 0, 0, 0.5); /* Black shadow with 50% transparency */

}

Using transparency effectively can enhance the visual appeal of your website and improve readability by allowing text or elements to partially show through backgrounds.

Color Picker Tools

To work with colors efficiently, you can use various color picker tools available online or integrated into code editors. These tools help you select and preview colors, generate corresponding CSS code, and manipulate color values with ease.

In summary, understanding different color notations and applying transparency to colors are essential skills for web designers and developers. CSS provides a variety of options to define and control colors, allowing you to create visually pleasing and dynamic web experiences. Whether you're choosing colors for text, backgrounds, or other design elements, having a solid grasp of color values and transparency can greatly impact the overall aesthetics of your website.

Section 4.2: Background Color and Images

Backgrounds play a crucial role in web design, setting the tone and style of a webpage. CSS provides extensive options for customizing background colors and images, allowing you to create visually appealing and engaging web experiences. In this section, we'll explore how to work with background colors and images in CSS.

Background Color

The background-color property in CSS allows you to set the background color of an element. You can specify colors using various notations, including named colors, hexadecimal values, RGB, RGBA, HSL, and HSLA, similar to how text colors are defined.

```css
/* Setting a background color using named color */

.header {

background-color: lightgray;

}

/* Setting a background color using hexadecimal value */

.navbar {

background-color: #007bff; /* A shade of blue */

}

/* Setting a background color using RGBA with transparency */

.section {

background-color: rgba(0, 128, 0, 0.5); /* Semi-transparent green */

}

/* Setting a background color using HSL */

.footer {

background-color: hsl(210, 100%, 50%); /* Pure green */

}
```

Choosing an appropriate background color is essential for creating a cohesive design and ensuring text and content remain readable. It's also important to consider accessibility guidelines when selecting background and text color combinations to ensure content is easily legible for all users.

Background Images

In addition to solid colors, CSS allows you to set background images for elements. This can be especially useful for creating visually rich designs, such as textured backgrounds or image overlays. You can use the background-image property to specify the image URL.

/* Setting a background image */

.header {

background-image: url('header-bg.jpg');

}

/* Using gradients as background images */

.section {

background-image: linear-gradient(45deg, #ff0000, #00ff00);

}

Background images can be either single images or gradients generated using the linear-gradient() or radial-gradient() functions. Gradients are versatile and allow you to create dynamic and colorful backgrounds without the need for image files.

Background Size and Position

CSS provides properties to control the size and position of background images. The background-size property allows you to specify how an image should be sized within its container, and the background-position property defines where the image should be positioned.

/* Controlling background image size and position */

```css
.section {

background-image: url('section-bg.jpg');

background-size: cover; /* Cover the entire container */

background-position: center; /* Center the image */

}

/* Using percentages for background size and position */

.article {

background-image: url('article-bg.jpg');

background-size: 50% auto; /* 50% width and auto height */

background-position: 20% 10%; /* 20% from left and 10% from top
*/

}
```

These properties allow you to fine-tune how background images are displayed, ensuring they fit the design and layout of your webpage.

Background Repeat and Attachment

The background-repeat property controls whether a background image should repeat (tile) both horizontally and vertically, only horizontally, only vertically, or not repeat at all. The background-attachment property determines whether the background image scrolls with the content or remains fixed within the viewport.

```css
/* Setting background repeat and attachment */

.section {
```

background-image: url('pattern-bg.png');

background-repeat: repeat-x; /* *Repeat only horizontally* */

background-attachment: fixed; /* *Fixed background* */

}

These properties give you control over how background images behave, allowing you to create visually interesting effects.

In summary, background colors and images are powerful tools in web design. CSS provides a wide range of options for customizing backgrounds, from setting solid colors to using images and gradients. Understanding how to control background size, position, repeat, and attachment is essential for creating visually appealing and engaging web layouts.

Section 4.3: Gradients and Patterns

Gradients and patterns are versatile tools in CSS that allow you to create visually appealing and textured backgrounds for your web elements. They can be used to add depth, dimension, and visual interest to your designs. In this section, we'll explore how to work with gradients and patterns in CSS.

Gradients

CSS gradients are a way to smoothly transition between two or more colors. They can be applied to backgrounds, text, borders, and more. Gradients are defined using the linear-gradient() or radial-gradient() function, and you can specify the direction, colors, and color stops.

Linear Gradients

Linear gradients create a smooth transition between two or more colors along a straight line. You can define the direction of the gradient using angles or keywords like "to top," "to bottom," "to left," or "to right."

```
/* Creating a horizontal linear gradient */

.button {

background: linear-gradient(to right, #ff6600, #ffcc00);

}

/* Creating a diagonal linear gradient */

.section {

background: linear-gradient(45deg, #3399ff, #ff3399);

}
```

In the first example, we create a horizontal gradient from left to right, transitioning from orange to yellow. In the second example, we create a diagonal gradient at a 45-degree angle, transitioning from blue to pink.

Radial Gradients

Radial gradients create a smooth transition from a starting color to an ending color radiating out from a central point. You can define the shape and size of the gradient using keywords and lengths.

```
/* Creating a circular radial gradient */
```

```css
.circle {

background: radial-gradient(circle, #33cc33, #ffcc00);

}

/* Creating an elliptical radial gradient */

.ellipse {

background: radial-gradient(ellipse at center, #990099, #ff3366);

}
```

In the first example, we create a circular gradient centered on the element, transitioning from green to yellow. In the second example, we create an elliptical gradient centered on the element, transitioning from purple to pink.

Background Patterns

Background patterns are repetitive designs that can be used to create textured backgrounds for web elements. CSS patterns can be created using a combination of background color, gradients, and repeating properties.

```css
/* Creating a striped background pattern */

.stripes {

background: repeating-linear-gradient(

-45deg,

#ffffff,

#ffffff 10px,
```

```
#33cc33 10px,

#33cc33 20px

);

}
```

/* Creating a checkered background pattern */

```
.checkerboard {

background:

linear-gradient(45deg, #ffffff 25%, transparent 25%),

linear-gradient(-45deg, #ffffff 25%, transparent 25%),

linear-gradient(45deg, transparent 75%, #ffffff 75%),

linear-gradient(-45deg, transparent 75%, #ffffff 75%);

background-size: 20px 20px;

}
```

In the first example, we create a striped pattern using a repeating linear gradient with alternating white and green stripes. In the second example, we create a checkered pattern using multiple linear gradients.

Patterns can be used to create visually interesting and unique backgrounds for various design elements, such as headers, buttons, or cards.

Gradient and Pattern Libraries

There are libraries and tools available that provide pre-designed gradients and patterns that you can easily incorporate into your CSS. These resources can save you time and effort when creating complex and aesthetically pleasing backgrounds.

In summary, gradients and patterns are valuable tools for enhancing the visual appeal of your web designs. CSS gradients allow you to smoothly transition between colors, while background patterns enable you to create textured and decorative backgrounds. Whether you want to add depth, dimension, or a unique style to your web elements, gradients and patterns offer creative possibilities for your design projects.

Section 4.4: CSS3 Shadows and Borders

CSS3 introduced advanced shadow and border properties that allow web designers to add depth, dimension, and visual effects to elements on a webpage. These properties provide more control and flexibility than their predecessors, enabling you to create stylish and immersive web designs. In this section, we'll explore CSS3 shadows and borders.

Box Shadows

The box-shadow property in CSS3 enables you to add shadow effects to elements. You can create shadows that appear both inside and outside of an element's borders. The box-shadow property accepts multiple values, allowing you to control the horizontal and vertical offset, blur radius, spread radius, color, and whether the shadow is inset or outset.

/ Creating an outer box shadow */*

```
.card {
```

box-shadow: 5px 5px 10px rgba(0, 0, 0, 0.3);

```
}
```

/* Creating an inner box shadow */

```
.button {
```

box-shadow: inset 0 0 5px rgba(0, 0, 0, 0.5);

```
}
```

In the first example, we add an outer shadow to a card element, giving it a subtle 10px blur. In the second example, we apply an inner shadow to a button element, making it appear pressed into the background.

Text Shadows

The text-shadow property in CSS3 allows you to add shadow effects specifically to text. You can create visually appealing text effects, such as text with a 3D look or glowing text.

/* Adding a text shadow to a heading */

```
h1 {
```

text-shadow: 2px 2px 4px rgba(0, 0, 0, 0.3);

```
}
```

/* Creating a neon text effect */

```
p.neon {
```

text-shadow: 0 0 5px #00ff00, 0 0 10px #00ff00, 0 0 15px #00ff00;

color: #00ff00;

}

In the first example, we apply a subtle text shadow to a heading, creating a slight 3D effect. In the second example, we create a neon text effect by applying multiple text shadows with different blurs and colors.

Border Radii

CSS3 introduced the border-radius property, which allows you to create rounded corners for elements. You can specify the radius for each corner individually, or use a single value for all corners.

/* Creating a button with rounded corners */

.button {

border-radius: 10px;

}

/* Applying different radii to each corner */

.card {

border-top-left-radius: 20px;

border-top-right-radius: 10px;

border-bottom-left-radius: 5px;

border-bottom-right-radius: 15px;

}

In the first example, we create a button with uniformly rounded corners. In the second example, we apply different radii to each corner of a card element, creating a more complex shape.

Border Images

The border-image property allows you to use an image as a border for an element instead of traditional border styles. You can control how the image is sliced and repeated to create custom border effects.

```
/* Using an image as a border */

.panel {

border-image: url('border.png') 20 repeat;

}
```

In this example, we apply an image as a border to a panel element, specifying the image URL, width of the border slices, and repetition pattern.

Gradient Borders

CSS3 also allows you to create gradient borders using the border-image property. This technique enables you to design borders with smooth color transitions.

```
/* Creating a gradient border */

.card {

border-image: linear-gradient(to right, #ff6600, #ffcc00) 1;

border-image-slice: 1;

}
```

In this example, we create a gradient border for a card element using a linear gradient. The border-image-slice property ensures that the entire border is filled with the gradient.

In summary, CSS3 shadows and borders provide powerful tools for enhancing the visual appearance of elements on a webpage. You can add depth, dimension, and stylish effects to your designs using box shadows, text shadows, rounded corners, border images, and gradient borders. These techniques enable you to create visually appealing and immersive web experiences.

Section 4.5: Creating Image Sprites for Performance

Image sprites are a technique used in web development to improve the performance and loading speed of websites. They involve combining multiple small images into a single image file, reducing the number of HTTP requests made to the server. In this section, we'll explore the concept of image sprites and how to create and use them effectively.

Understanding Image Sprites

In a typical web page, various elements like icons, buttons, and other small graphics are often represented as separate image files. When a user visits the page, the browser makes a separate HTTP request for each of these images. This can lead to slower page loading times, especially on slower network connections.

Image sprites address this issue by combining multiple images into one larger image file. Instead of downloading several small files individually, the browser fetches a single sprite image. CSS is then used to display specific parts of the sprite in the appropriate locations on the page.

Creating Image Sprites

To create an image sprite, you'll need to follow these steps:

1. **Gather Your Images**: Collect all the small images (icons, buttons, etc.) that you want to include in the sprite.
2. **Arrange Them**: Arrange the images in a grid within a single image file. You can use image editing tools like Photoshop or online sprite generators for this purpose. Ensure that there is enough spacing between images to prevent unintended overlap.
3. **Save the Sprite**: Save the combined image file, typically in a format like PNG or JPEG.
4. **Use CSS to Display Specific Images**: In your CSS, specify the sprite as a background image for elements and use the background-position property to display the specific image from the sprite.

```
/* Using a sprite for a button */

.button {

width: 32px;

height: 32px;

background-image: url('sprite.png');

background-position: -64px -32px; /* Adjust to display the desired image */

}
```

Advantages of Image Sprites

Using image sprites offers several advantages:

1. **Reduced HTTP Requests**: By consolidating multiple images into one, you reduce the number of server requests, leading to faster page loading times.
2. **Improved Performance**: Smaller HTTP requests mean quicker rendering of web pages, which is particularly important on mobile devices and for users with slower internet connections.
3. **Simplified Maintenance**: Managing a single sprite image is easier than handling numerous individual image files, simplifying maintenance and updates.
4. **Caching Benefits**: Sprites can be cached by the browser, improving load times for subsequent visits to the same website.

Best Practices

When working with image sprites, consider the following best practices:

1. **Optimize Images**: Optimize the individual images within the sprite to minimize file size while maintaining quality.
2. **Use Consistent Sizing**: Ensure that all images in the sprite have consistent dimensions, which makes positioning them accurately in CSS easier.
3. **Document and Organize**: Keep track of the position and dimensions of each image in your sprite, as well as their purpose, to make maintenance easier.
4. **Generate Retina Sprites**: For high-resolution displays, create separate sprites with higher-resolution images and use media queries to load the appropriate sprite.
5. **Consider Accessibility**: Ensure that the images you use from the sprite are accessible to all users, including those who rely on screen readers. Use appropriate alt text and

ARIA roles where necessary.

In conclusion, image sprites are a valuable technique for improving web performance by reducing the number of HTTP requests and speeding up page loading times. By combining multiple small images into a single sprite and using CSS to display specific parts of it, you can create faster and more efficient websites while maintaining a visually appealing design.

Chapter 5: Layouts with CSS Flexbox

Section 5.1: Introduction to Flexbox

CSS Flexbox, or Flexible Box Layout, is a powerful layout model introduced in CSS3 that simplifies the design and alignment of complex web layouts. Flexbox allows you to create flexible and responsive designs with ease, making it a valuable tool for modern web development. In this section, we'll introduce you to the fundamentals of Flexbox and how it works.

What Is Flexbox?

Flexbox is a one-dimensional layout model, meaning it deals with either rows or columns, but not both at the same time. It is designed to distribute space along a single axis while ensuring that elements maintain their desired proportions and alignment relative to one another. Flexbox excels at aligning elements within a container, making it particularly suitable for creating responsive and evenly spaced layouts.

Flex Containers and Flex Items

In Flexbox, there are two primary roles:

1. **Flex Container**: The parent element that contains one or more child elements (flex items). To create a flex container, you apply the display: flex; or display: inline-flex; property to it.

/ Creating a flex container */*

.flex-container {

display: flex;

}

1. **Flex Items**: The child elements within a flex container. These are the elements that will be arranged and aligned according to the flex container's rules.

/* Styling flex items */

.flex-item {

flex: 1; /* Adjust the flex property to control item sizing */

}

Main Axis and Cross Axis

In Flexbox, the layout revolves around two axes:

1. **Main Axis**: The primary axis along which flex items are laid out within the flex container. It can be either horizontal (left-to-right) or vertical (top-to-bottom) based on the container's orientation.
2. **Cross Axis**: The orthogonal axis perpendicular to the main axis. It runs across the main axis. If the main axis is horizontal, the cross axis is vertical, and vice versa.

Flexbox Properties

Flexbox introduces several properties to control the layout and alignment of flex containers and items. Some of the key properties include:

- flex-direction: Determines the main axis direction (row or column).

• justify-content: Defines how items are distributed along the main axis.

• align-items: Specifies how items are aligned on the cross axis.

• align-content: Controls the alignment of lines (rows or columns) on the cross axis when there is extra space available.

Flex Values

The flex property is crucial in Flexbox and is used to define the ability of a flex item to expand or shrink relative to the other items. It consists of three values: flex-grow, flex-shrink, and flex-basis.

/ Example of the flex property */*

.flex-item {

flex: 1 1 200px;

}

In the example above, flex: 1 1 200px; means the item can grow (flex-grow: 1), shrink (flex-shrink: 1), and its initial size is 200 pixels (flex-basis: 200px).

Responsive Design with Flexbox

Flexbox is excellent for creating responsive designs because it allows elements to adapt to various screen sizes and orientations automatically. By adjusting the flex properties, you can control how flex items behave and rearrange themselves as the available space changes.

In summary, Flexbox is a powerful layout model in CSS that simplifies the design and alignment of web layouts. It revolves around the concept of flex containers and flex items, with properties to control the layout along the main and cross axes. Flexbox is particularly useful for creating responsive and evenly spaced layouts, making it an essential tool for modern web development.

Section 5.2: Flex Container and Flex Items

In Flexbox layout, elements are organized within a flex container, and their arrangement and alignment are controlled by the properties applied to this container and its child elements, known as flex items. In this section, we will dive deeper into the concepts of flex containers and flex items, exploring how they work together to create flexible layouts.

Creating a Flex Container

To create a flex container, you need to apply the display: flex; property to an HTML element. This element will serve as the parent container for the flex items. Once you designate an element as a flex container, it will automatically become the main axis along which the flex items are aligned.

```css
/* Creating a flex container */

.container {

display: flex;

}
```

Flex Items Inside a Container

Any direct child element of a flex container becomes a flex item. These flex items will be arranged and aligned within the container according to the rules you define. By default, flex items flow in a row from left to right, but you can change this behavior using the flex-direction property.

/* Styling flex items */

.item {

flex: 1; /* Adjust the flex property to control item sizing */

}

In the example above, the .item class is applied to flex items within the .container. The flex property controls how much space each item should take relative to others.

The Main Axis and Cross Axis

Understanding the main axis and cross axis is essential when working with Flexbox. The main axis is the primary direction in which flex items are laid out. It can be horizontal (from left to right) or vertical (from top to bottom) depending on the flex-direction property.

The cross axis is perpendicular to the main axis. If the main axis is horizontal, the cross axis is vertical, and vice versa. Alignment properties like align-items and align-content control how items are positioned on the cross axis.

Justifying Content

The justify-content property defines how flex items are distributed along the main axis within the container. It allows you to control the spacing between items or how they are positioned within the available space.

/ Justifying content */*

.container {

display: flex;

justify-content: space-between; */* Distribute items evenly with space between */*

}

In the example above, justify-content: space-between; evenly distributes the flex items along the main axis, with equal space between them.

Aligning Items

The align-items property is used to align flex items along the cross axis within the flex container. It determines how items are positioned vertically (if the main axis is horizontal) or horizontally (if the main axis is vertical).

/ Aligning items vertically */*

.container {

display: flex;

align-items: center; */* Center items vertically */*

}

In this example, align-items: center; vertically centers the flex items within the container.

Wrapping Flex Items

By default, flex items will try to fit in a single line, causing them to shrink or overflow the container if there isn't enough space. You can control this behavior using the flex-wrap property.

```css
/* Wrapping flex items */

.container {

display: flex;

flex-wrap: wrap; /* Allow items to wrap to the next line */

}
```

Setting flex-wrap: wrap; allows flex items to wrap to the next line when they don't fit horizontally in the container.

Nested Flex Containers

Flexbox can be nested, allowing you to create more complex layouts. In a nested structure, each flex container acts independently, with its own main and cross axes. This nesting provides a powerful way to achieve sophisticated designs while maintaining flexibility and control.

```html
<div class="outer-container">

<div class="inner-container">

<!--Nested flex container and items-->

</div>

</div>
```

In the example above, the .inner-container is a flex container nested inside the .outer-container.

In summary, Flexbox relies on the concept of flex containers and flex items to create flexible layouts. The properties applied to the flex container and its items determine how elements are arranged and aligned along the main and cross axes. Understanding these principles is crucial for building responsive and well-organized web layouts.

Section 5.3: Flex Direction and Alignment

In the Flexbox layout model, the flex-direction property plays a central role in determining the direction in which flex items are arranged within a flex container. Additionally, alignment properties help control how these items are positioned along the main and cross axes. In this section, we'll explore the flex-direction property and various alignment options to achieve the desired layout.

flex-direction Property

The flex-direction property defines the primary axis along which flex items are laid out within a flex container. It can take one of four values:

1. row (default): Flex items are arranged in a row from left to right (for LTR languages) or right to left (for RTL languages).

.container {

display: flex;

flex-direction: row;

```
}
```

1. row-reverse: Flex items are arranged in a row but in reverse order.

```
.container {

display: flex;

flex-direction: row-reverse;

}
```

1. column: Flex items are arranged in a column from top to bottom.

```
.container {

display: flex;

flex-direction: column;

}
```

1. column-reverse: Flex items are arranged in a column but in reverse order.

```
.container {

display: flex;

flex-direction: column-reverse;

}
```

By adjusting the flex-direction property, you can easily switch between horizontal and vertical layouts or reverse the order of elements within the container.

Main Axis and Cross Axis Alignment

Once you've set the flex-direction, you can control how flex items are aligned along the main and cross axes using alignment properties. These properties include:

- justify-content: Controls the alignment of items along the main axis.

- align-items: Specifies how items are aligned on the cross axis.

- align-self: Allows individual items to override the align-items value for custom alignment.

justify-content Property

The justify-content property determines how flex items are distributed along the main axis. It affects the spacing between items and their positioning within the container. It can take one of the following values:

- flex-start (default): Items are packed at the start of the main axis.

.container {

display: flex;

justify-content: flex-start;

}

- flex-end: Items are packed at the end of the main axis.

.container {

display: flex;

justify-content: flex-end;

}

- center: Items are centered along the main axis.

.container {

display: flex;

justify-content: center;

}

- space-between: Items are evenly distributed along the main axis with space between them.

.container {

display: flex;

justify-content: space-between;

}

- space-around: Items are evenly distributed along the main axis with space around them.

.container {

display: flex;

justify-content: space-around;

}

- space-evenly: Items are evenly distributed along the main axis with equal space between and around them.

.container {

display: flex;

justify-content: space-evenly;

}

align-items Property

The align-items property controls how flex items are aligned on the cross axis within the flex container. It can take one of the following values:

- stretch (default): Items are stretched to fill the container's cross-axis dimension.

.container {

display: flex;

align-items: stretch;

}

- flex-start: Items are aligned at the start of the cross axis.

.container {

```css
display: flex;

align-items: flex-start;

}
```

- flex-end: Items are aligned at the end of the cross axis.

```css
.container {

display: flex;

align-items: flex-end;

}
```

- center: Items are centered along the cross axis.

```css
.container {

display: flex;

align-items: center;

}
```

align-self Property

The align-self property allows you to individually control the alignment of specific flex items within the container. It can take the same values as align-items and overrides the alignment for that particular item.

```css
/* Aligning a specific item to the end of the cross axis */

.item {
```

align-self: flex-end;

}

In summary, the flex-direction property defines the primary axis along which flex items are arranged in a flex container. You can control item alignment along the main and cross axes using properties like justify-content, align-items, and align-self. Understanding how to manipulate these properties is essential for creating flexible and responsive layouts using Flexbox.

Section 5.4: Flexbox for Responsive Design

Flexbox is a versatile layout model that excels at creating responsive web designs. Its ability to automatically adapt to various screen sizes and orientations makes it a valuable tool for modern web development. In this section, we'll explore how Flexbox can be used to achieve responsive layouts and handle different devices effectively.

Responsive Design Basics

Responsive web design aims to provide an optimal user experience on a wide range of devices and screen sizes. It involves fluid layouts, flexible images, and media queries to ensure that web content looks and functions well regardless of the device used. Flexbox plays a crucial role in creating these fluid layouts.

Fluid Layouts with Flexbox

One of the key features of Flexbox is its ability to create fluid layouts without relying on fixed widths or heights. By setting the appropriate flex properties, you can allow elements to automatically adjust their sizes based on available space.

/ Creating a fluid layout with Flexbox */*

```
.container {

display: flex;

flex-wrap: wrap;

}

.item {

flex: 1; /* Each item takes an equal portion of available space */

min-width: 200px; /* Define a minimum width to prevent items from
becoming too narrow */

}
```

In this example, the .container is a flex container, and .item elements automatically adjust their widths based on the container's size. The flex: 1; property ensures that each item takes an equal portion of available space.

Media Queries and Flex Direction

Media queries are essential for responsive design. They allow you to apply different styles and layouts based on the device's screen size and characteristics. Flexbox can be combined with media queries to change the direction of the main axis, adapting the layout as needed.

```
/* Adjusting flex direction in a media query */

.container {

display: flex;

flex-wrap: wrap;

}
```

```
@media screen and (max-width: 768px) {

.container {

flex-direction: column; /* Switch to a column layout on smaller
screens */

}

}
```

In this example, when the screen width is 768 pixels or less, the flex direction changes to column, creating a vertically stacked layout. This responsive adjustment ensures better readability on smaller screens.

Flexbox for Navigation Menus

Flexbox is particularly useful for creating responsive navigation menus. By setting up a flex container for your menu items, you can easily adjust their arrangement as the screen size changes.

```
/* Creating a responsive navigation menu with Flexbox */

.nav {

display: flex;

justify-content: space-between; /* Distribute menu items evenly */

}

.menu-item {

margin: 0 10px; /* Add spacing between menu items */

}

@media screen and (max-width: 768px) {
```

```
.nav {
```

flex-direction: column; /* *Switch to a vertical layout on smaller screens* */

align-items: center; /* *Center items horizontally* */

```
}
```

```
.menu-item {
```

margin: 10px 0; /* *Adjust vertical spacing* */

```
}
```

```
}
```

In this example, the navigation menu adjusts its layout when the screen width is 768 pixels or less. It switches to a vertical layout with centered items for better usability on small screens.

Flexbox for Card Layouts

Card layouts are commonly used in web design, and Flexbox simplifies the creation of responsive card grids. You can use a combination of flex containers and flex items to achieve a grid of cards that adapt to different screen sizes.

/* *Creating a responsive card grid with Flexbox* */

```
.card-container {
```

display: flex;

flex-wrap: wrap;

justify-content: space-between; /* *Distribute cards evenly* */

```
}

.card {

    flex: 1; /* Each card takes an equal portion of available space */

    min-width: 300px; /* Define a minimum card width */

}

@media screen and (max-width: 768px) {

    .card {

        min-width: 100%; /* Cards span the full width on smaller screens */

    }

}
```

In this example, the .card-container is a flex container, and .card elements automatically adjust their widths based on available space. When the screen width is 768 pixels or less, the cards span the full width for better responsiveness.

In conclusion, Flexbox is an excellent choice for creating responsive web designs. Its ability to create fluid layouts, combined with media queries for responsive adjustments, makes it a valuable tool for handling different devices effectively. Whether you're designing navigation menus, card layouts, or complex web pages, Flexbox provides the flexibility needed for a responsive user experience.

Section 5.5: Advanced Flexbox Techniques

In addition to the fundamental concepts covered in previous sections, Flexbox offers several advanced techniques and features that can help you create more complex and finely-tuned layouts.

In this section, we'll explore some of these advanced Flexbox techniques and how they can be applied in your web development projects.

Ordering Flex Items

Flexbox allows you to control the order in which flex items appear within the flex container, independently of their source order in the HTML. The order property is used to define the order of items, with lower values appearing first.

/* Changing the order of flex items */

.item-1 {

order: 3; /* This item appears third in the layout */

}

.item-2 {

order: 1; /* This item appears first in the layout */

}

.item-3 {

order: 2; /* This item appears second in the layout */

}

In this example, the order property determines the order in which item-1, item-2, and item-3 appear, regardless of their HTML source order. Lower values result in items appearing earlier in the layout.

Flexbox Alignment in Cross Axis

While we've discussed aligning items on the cross axis using align-items, you can fine-tune alignment for individual items using the align-self property. This property allows you to override the alignment set by align-items for specific items.

/ Custom alignment for a flex item */*

.item {

align-self: flex-end; */* This item is aligned to the end on the cross axis */*

}

By applying align-self to specific items, you can achieve custom alignment within a flex container.

Creating Flexbox Tooltips

Flexbox can be used creatively to create tooltips without relying on JavaScript or additional HTML elements. By using a combination of position: relative and position: absolute, you can position tooltip content relative to a parent element.

/ Creating a Flexbox tooltip */*

.parent {

position: relative;

}

.tooltip {

position: absolute;

bottom: 100%;

left: 50%;

transform: translateX(-50%);

background-color: #333;

color: #fff;

padding: 5px;

border-radius: 4px;

display: none;

}

.parent:*hover* .tooltip {

display: block;

}

In this example, the .parent element contains a hidden tooltip with the class .tooltip. When the parent is hovered over, the tooltip becomes visible, creating a simple tooltip effect using Flexbox.

Flexbox for Masonry Grids

Masonry grids, where items have varying heights and are arranged optimally, can be challenging to implement with CSS alone. Flexbox can be a useful tool for creating masonry-style layouts.

/* Creating a Flexbox masonry grid */

.masonry-container {

display: flex;

```
flex-wrap: wrap;

}

.masonry-item {

flex: 1;

margin: 5px; /* Add spacing between items */

}
```

By using a combination of flex properties and margin spacing, you can achieve a masonry-style grid layout without complex JavaScript or additional libraries.

Equal Height Columns with Flexbox

Equalizing the height of columns in a grid is a common layout requirement. Flexbox simplifies this task by allowing columns to automatically adjust their heights based on content.

```
/* Creating equal height columns with Flexbox */

.column-container {

display: flex;

}

.column {

flex: 1;

margin: 5px; /* Add spacing between columns */

}
```

In this example, the columns within the .column-container automatically have equal heights, making it easier to create grid-like layouts without using hacks or JavaScript.

Wrapping and Breaking Flex Items

By default, flex items will try to fit in a single line, causing them to shrink or overflow the container if there isn't enough space. However, you can control this behavior using the flex-wrap property.

/* Wrapping and breaking flex items */

.container {

display: flex;

flex-wrap: wrap; /* Allow items to wrap to the next line */

}

Setting flex-wrap: wrap; allows flex items to wrap to the next line when they don't fit horizontally in the container. This can be useful for creating responsive designs with variable content.

In summary, Flexbox offers advanced techniques and features that can enhance your web layouts. These techniques include ordering flex items, custom alignment using align-self, creating tooltips, masonry-style grids, equal height columns, and controlling item wrapping and breaking. By mastering these advanced Flexbox concepts, you can create more sophisticated and responsive designs for your web projects.

Chapter 6: Building Responsive Designs with CSS Grid

Section 6.1: Understanding CSS Grid Layout

CSS Grid Layout, often referred to simply as Grid, is a powerful two-dimensional layout system that allows you to create complex grid-based layouts with ease. Unlike Flexbox, which is primarily designed for one-dimensional layouts, Grid is designed for both rows and columns. It provides precise control over the placement and alignment of items within the grid container.

Creating a Grid Container

To get started with CSS Grid, you need to define a grid container. You can do this by applying the display: grid; property to an element. Once an element becomes a grid container, it can contain grid items.

/* Creating a grid container */

.container {

display: grid;

}

In this example, the .container element becomes a grid container.

Grid Rows and Columns

Grid layouts consist of rows and columns. You can define the number and size of rows and columns using various properties. The most common properties for this purpose are grid-template-rows and grid-template-columns.

```css
/* Defining grid rows and columns */

.container {

display: grid;

grid-template-rows: 1fr 2fr; /* Two rows with a 1:2 ratio */

grid-template-columns: 50% 30% 20%; /* Three columns with
specified widths */

}
```

In this example, we create a grid with two rows and three columns, each with a specific size or ratio.

Placing Grid Items

Grid items are the elements that reside within a grid container. You can place grid items into specific cells of the grid using the grid-row and grid-column properties.

```css
/* Placing grid items */

.item1 {

grid-row: 1 / 2; /* Start in row 1 and end in row 2 */

grid-column: 2 / 4; /* Start in column 2 and end in column 4 */

}
```

In this example, item1 is placed in the first row (from row 1 to row 2) and spans from the second column to the fourth column.

Grid Gaps and Gutters

Grid layouts often have gaps or gutters between rows and columns. You can control the spacing between grid items using the grid-gap property.

```
/* Adding gaps between grid items */

.container {

display: grid;

grid-gap: 10px; /* 10px gap between grid items */

}
```

In this example, a 10px gap is added between grid items within the grid container.

Responsive Grids with Media Queries

One of the strengths of CSS Grid is its ability to create responsive layouts easily. By using media queries, you can change the grid's structure and behavior based on screen size or other conditions.

```
/* Creating a responsive grid */

.container {

display: grid;

grid-template-columns: 1fr 1fr; /* Two columns by default */

@media (min-width: 768px) {

grid-template-columns: 1fr 1fr 1fr; /* Three columns for larger screens */
```

```
}

}
```

In this example, the grid changes from two columns to three columns when the screen width is 768px or larger.

CSS Grid Browser Support

CSS Grid is well-supported in modern browsers. However, if you need to ensure compatibility with older browsers, you can use feature detection and provide fallback layouts or use other layout methods for unsupported browsers.

In summary, CSS Grid Layout is a versatile and powerful tool for creating complex and responsive grid-based layouts. It allows you to define grid containers, rows, columns, and gaps, and it provides precise control over the placement of grid items. When combined with media queries, CSS Grid enables you to create layouts that adapt to different screen sizes and devices, making it a valuable addition to your web design toolkit.

Section 6.2: Creating Grid Containers and Grid Items

In the previous section, we explored the fundamentals of CSS Grid Layout and how to set up a grid container with rows and columns. In this section, we will delve deeper into creating grid containers and placing grid items within them.

Creating Nested Grids

CSS Grid allows you to nest grids within other grids, creating complex layouts. This feature is particularly useful when you want to create subsections of your layout with their own grid structures. To create a nested grid, you simply define another element within a grid item and apply the display: grid; property to it.

/ Creating a nested grid */*

.container {

display: grid;

grid-template-columns: 1fr 1fr;

grid-gap: 10px;

}

.item1 {

/ Nested grid within item1 */*

display: grid;

grid-template-columns: 1fr 2fr;

grid-gap: 5px;

}

In this example, we have a parent grid container (.container) with two columns and a 10px gap. Inside the first grid item (.item1), we create a nested grid with two columns and a 5px gap. This allows for fine-grained control of the layout within the .item1 grid.

Grid Lines and Template Areas

CSS Grid also provides a convenient way to define the structure of your grid using named grid lines and template areas. You can name grid lines to reference them later when placing grid items. Template areas allow you to visually define the placement of items within the grid.

```css
/* Defining grid lines and template areas */

.container {

display: grid;

grid-template-columns: 1fr 1fr;

grid-template-rows: auto 1fr;

grid-template-areas:

"header header"

"sidebar main";

}
.header {

grid-area: header;

}
.sidebar {

grid-area: sidebar;

}
.main {

grid-area: main;

}
```

In this example, we define a grid with two columns and two rows, along with named grid areas for the header, sidebar, and main content. By assigning the grid-area property to the respective grid items, we place them in their designated areas.

Auto-Sizing Grid Tracks

CSS Grid provides a powerful feature called "auto-sizing," which allows grid tracks (rows or columns) to automatically adjust their size based on content or available space. This is particularly useful for creating flexible layouts.

/* Auto-sizing grid tracks */

.container {

display: grid;

grid-template-columns: 1fr auto;

grid-template-rows: auto 1fr;

}

In this example, the second column and second row are set to auto, which means they will size themselves based on their content. This can be handy when you have variable content within grid items.

Grid Item Placement

Placing grid items within a grid container can be done using various properties like grid-row, grid-column, grid-area, and grid-template-areas. You can also use shorthand notations to define both row and column placement.

/* Placing grid items */

```
.item1 {

grid-row: 1 / 2; /* Starts in row 1 and ends in row 2 */

grid-column: 2 / 3; /* Starts in column 2 and ends in column 3 */

}

.item2 {

grid-area: header; /* Places the item in the "header" named area */

}
```

In this snippet, we place item1 by specifying its starting and ending row and column. For item2, we use the grid-area property to place it in the named "header" area.

CSS Grid and Responsive Design

One of the strengths of CSS Grid is its compatibility with responsive design. You can use media queries to adjust the grid structure, change the number of columns, or even switch between different grid layouts for different screen sizes.

```
/* Responsive grid layout */

.container {

display: grid;

grid-template-columns: 1fr;

@media (min-width: 768px) {

grid-template-columns: 1fr 1fr;

}
```

}

In this example, the grid switches from a single column layout to a two-column layout when the screen width reaches 768px or larger. This flexibility makes CSS Grid a powerful tool for creating responsive web designs.

In summary, CSS Grid allows you to create sophisticated layouts by nesting grids, defining grid lines and template areas, and using auto-sizing for tracks. You can precisely place grid items within a grid container using various properties, and CSS Grid seamlessly integrates with responsive design techniques to adapt to different screen sizes.

Section 6.3: Grid Lines and Template Areas

CSS Grid Layout offers powerful features for creating complex grid-based layouts with ease. In this section, we will explore the concept of grid lines and template areas, which provide a flexible and visual way to define the structure of your grid.

Defining Grid Lines

Grid lines are imaginary lines that divide the grid container into rows and columns. These lines serve as reference points for placing grid items. You can explicitly define grid lines using the grid-template-rows and grid-template-columns properties.

/* *Defining grid lines* */

.container {

display: grid;

grid-template-rows: 1fr 2fr; /* *Two rows with a 1:2 ratio* */

grid-template-columns: 50% 30% 20%; /* *Three columns with specified widths* */

}

In this example, we define two rows and three columns. The grid-template-rows property creates two rows with a 1:2 height ratio, while the grid-template-columns property defines three columns with specific width percentages.

Named Grid Lines

Grid lines can also be named, making it easier to reference them when placing grid items. You can name grid lines by using square brackets and providing a name inside them.

/* *Named grid lines* */

.container {

display: grid;

grid-template-rows: [header-start] 100px [header-end main-start] 1fr [main-end];

grid-template-columns: [sidebar-start] 200px [sidebar-end content-start] 1fr [content-end];

}

In this example, we define named grid lines such as header-start, header-end, main-start, main-end, sidebar-start, sidebar-end, content-start, and content-end. These names can be used later to place grid items precisely.

Template Areas

Template areas provide a visual way to define the layout of your grid by naming rectangular regions. You can assign names to areas using the grid-template-areas property, which takes a string that represents the grid layout.

/* Template areas */

.container {

display: grid;

grid-template-rows: auto 1fr auto;

grid-template-columns: 1fr 2fr;

grid-template-areas:

"header header"

"sidebar main"

"footer footer";

}

In this example, we define a grid with three rows and two columns. The grid-template-areas property assigns names to areas in a grid layout. Grid items can then be placed into these named areas using the grid-area property.

Placing Grid Items in Named Areas

To place grid items within named areas, you can use the grid-area property with the name of the desired area.

/* Placing grid items in named areas */

```
.header {

grid-area: header;

}

.main {

grid-area: main;

}

.sidebar {

grid-area: sidebar;

}

.footer {

grid-area: footer;

}
```

In this snippet, we assign grid items to their respective named areas within the grid container. This approach provides a clear and readable way to define the layout of your webpage.

Responsive Grid Layout with Template Areas

One of the advantages of using named grid areas and template areas is their compatibility with responsive design. By changing the template areas within media queries, you can adapt your grid layout to different screen sizes.

```
/* Responsive grid layout with template areas */

.container {
```

display: grid;

grid-template-rows: auto 1fr auto;

grid-template-columns: 1fr 2fr;

@media (**max-width**: 768px) {

grid-template-areas:

"header header"

"main main"

"sidebar sidebar"

"footer footer";

}

}

In this example, we adjust the template areas for smaller screens, rearranging the layout to better suit the available space. This flexibility makes CSS Grid a versatile choice for responsive web design.

In summary, CSS Grid Layout provides an efficient way to create grid-based layouts with grid lines and named template areas. Grid lines help define the structure of the grid, and named areas provide a visual representation of the layout. This approach simplifies the placement of grid items and allows for responsive design adjustments by changing template areas within media queries.

Section 6.4: Responsive Grids with Media Queries

Creating responsive web designs that adapt to various screen sizes is a crucial aspect of modern web development. CSS Grid Layout offers a powerful toolset for building flexible and responsive grid-based layouts. In this section, we will explore how to create responsive grids using media queries and CSS Grid.

Understanding Media Queries

Media queries are a CSS feature that allows you to apply different styles to a webpage based on the characteristics of the user's device, such as screen width, height, or orientation. They are commonly used for responsive web design.

```
/* Example of a media query */

@media (max-width: 768px) {

/* CSS rules to apply when the screen width is 768px or less */

.container {

grid-template-columns: 1fr;

}

}
```

In this example, a media query is used to apply specific CSS rules to the .container element when the screen width is 768 pixels or less. This enables you to customize the layout for smaller screens.

Adapting Grid Layouts with Media Queries

To create responsive grids with CSS Grid, you can use media queries to adjust grid properties, such as the number of columns, column widths, or grid templates. Here's an example of how you can adapt a grid layout for different screen sizes:

```css
/* Initial grid layout */

.container {

display: grid;

grid-template-columns: repeat(3, 1fr);

grid-gap: 20px;

}

/* Media query for smaller screens */

@media (max-width: 768px) {

.container {

grid-template-columns: repeat(2, 1fr);

}

}
```

In this code, the initial grid layout consists of three columns. However, when the screen width is 768 pixels or less, the media query adjusts the grid to have two columns instead.

Changing Grid Templates

Media queries can also be used to completely change the grid template for different screen sizes. This allows for more significant layout modifications.

```
/* Default grid layout */

.container {

display: grid;

grid-template-columns: 1fr 1fr 1fr;

}

/* Media query for smaller screens */

@media (max-width: 480px) {

.container {

grid-template-columns: 1fr;

}

}
```

In this example, the default grid layout has three columns, but when the screen width becomes 480 pixels or less, the media query changes it to a single column layout.

Complex Responsive Grids

Responsive grid design can become more complex as your layout requirements evolve. You may need to consider reordering grid items, changing grid areas, or adjusting spacing between items to optimize the user experience on different devices.

```css
/* Complex responsive grid example */

.container {

display: grid;

grid-template-columns: 1fr 1fr 1fr;

grid-template-rows: auto;

grid-gap: 20px;

}

@media (max-width: 768px) {

.container {

grid-template-columns: 1fr;

}

.item-1 {

grid-row: 1;

}

.item-2 {

grid-row: 2;

}

.item-3 {

grid-row: 3;

}
```

}

In this complex example, the grid layout is initially divided into three columns, but on smaller screens, it becomes a single column layout. Additionally, specific grid items are repositioned using the grid-row property within the media query.

Testing and Debugging

Testing your responsive grid design across various devices and screen sizes is essential to ensure a consistent and user-friendly experience. Browser developer tools offer responsive design modes that allow you to preview your layout on different devices. Regular testing and debugging help identify and address any layout issues that may arise.

In summary, creating responsive grids with CSS Grid Layout involves using media queries to adjust grid properties and layouts based on screen size. By understanding and utilizing media queries effectively, you can build adaptable and user-friendly grid-based layouts for a wide range of devices and screen resolutions.

Section 6.5: CSS Grid Best Practices

When working with CSS Grid Layout, following best practices can help you create efficient, maintainable, and responsive grid-based layouts. In this section, we'll explore some essential CSS Grid best practices to ensure your grid designs are optimized.

1. Start with a Clear Grid Structure

Define your grid structure with a clear understanding of the layout you want to achieve. Plan the number of rows and columns, as well as their sizes, before implementing the grid. Having a well-thought-out structure simplifies the layout process and makes your code more maintainable.

/* Define a clear grid structure */

.container {

display: grid;

grid-template-columns: repeat(3, 1fr);

grid-template-rows: 100px auto 200px;

}

2. Use Named Grid Areas

Assign names to grid areas using the grid-template-areas property. Named grid areas provide a visual representation of your layout and make it easier to place grid items precisely within the grid.

/* Use named grid areas for clarity */

.container {

display: grid;

grid-template-columns: 1fr 2fr;

grid-template-areas:

"header header"

"sidebar main"

"footer footer";

}

3. Embrace Responsive Design

Utilize media queries to create responsive grid layouts that adapt to various screen sizes. Adjust the number of columns or change the grid template to optimize the user experience on different devices.

```
/* Create responsive grid layouts with media queries */

@media (max-width: 768px) {

.container {

grid-template-columns: 1fr;

}

}
```

4. Maintain Consistency

Maintain consistent gutter spacing between grid items using the grid-gap property. Consistency in spacing enhances the visual appeal of your layout and improves readability.

```
/* Maintain consistent gutter spacing */

.container {

display: grid;

grid-gap: 20px;

}
```

5. Leverage Auto Placement

Let the grid automatically place items using the grid-auto-flow property. This is especially useful when dealing with dynamic content or items of varying sizes.

```
/* Leverage auto placement for flexibility */

.container {

display: grid;

grid-auto-flow: dense;

}
```

6. Handle Grid Item Alignment

Control the alignment of grid items within their cells using properties like justify-self and align-self. These properties allow you to fine-tune the position of individual items.

```
/* Align grid items as needed */

.item-1 {

justify-self: start;

align-self: center;

}
```

7. Test and Debug

Regularly test your grid layouts across different devices and browsers to identify and resolve layout issues. Browser developer tools provide responsive design modes that make testing more accessible.

8. Keep Accessibility in Mind

Ensure your grid layouts are accessible to all users. Use semantic HTML elements and ARIA roles to provide meaningful structure and labeling to assistive technologies.

9. Document Your Code

Add comments and documentation to your CSS code to make it more understandable and maintainable. Document the purpose of grid areas, breakpoints, and any custom classes or IDs used in your layout.

10. Stay Informed

Stay up-to-date with CSS Grid specifications and best practices. CSS Grid is continually evolving, and new features and techniques may become available to improve your grid layouts.

By following these CSS Grid best practices, you can create responsive and well-structured grid-based layouts that enhance the user experience and make your code easier to maintain and debug.

Chapter 7: CSS Transitions and Animations

Section 7.1: CSS Transitions: Basics and Properties

CSS transitions allow you to smoothly change the property values of elements over a specified duration, creating visually appealing effects without JavaScript. Transitions are commonly used for hover effects, menu animations, and other interactive elements on websites. In this section, we'll dive into the basics of CSS transitions and explore the properties that control them.

Understanding Transitions

A CSS transition consists of a property, a duration, a timing function, and a delay. Here's the syntax:

/* Syntax for CSS transitions */

element {

transition: property duration timing-function delay;

}

- property: Specifies the CSS property you want to transition (e.g., color, width, opacity).

- duration: Determines how long the transition takes to complete (e.g., 0.5s for half a second).

- timing-function: Defines the acceleration curve for the transition (e.g., ease, linear, ease-in-out).

- delay: Optionally sets a delay before the transition starts (e.g., 0.2s for a 0.2-second delay).

Simple Transition Example

Let's start with a simple example. Suppose you want to change the text color of a button smoothly when a user hovers over it:

/ CSS for a button with a color transition */*

.button {

background-color: #3498db;

color: #fff;

transition: color 0.3s ease;

}

.button:*hover* {

color: #e74c3c;

}

In this code, the color property of the .button element will transition smoothly over 0.3 seconds with an easing timing function when the user hovers over it. The color changes from white to a shade of red when the hover state is activated.

Common Transition Properties

CSS transitions can be applied to various properties, such as width, height, opacity, and more. Here are some common properties and their usage:

- **Width and Height**: Transitioning the dimensions of elements can create smooth resizing effects.

```
/* Transitioning width and height */

.box {

width: 100px;

height: 100px;

transition: width 0.3s ease, height 0.3s ease;

}

.box:hover {

width: 200px;

height: 200px;

}
```

- **Opacity**: Transitioning opacity is useful for creating fade-in and fade-out effects.

```
/* Transitioning opacity */

.fade-in {

opacity: 0;

transition: opacity 0.5s ease;

}
```

```
.fade-in:hover {

opacity: 1;

}
```

- **Transform**: Transitioning transformations like scale, rotate, and translate can add dynamic animations.

```
/* Transitioning transform */

.rotate {

transform: rotate(0deg);

transition: transform 0.5s ease;

}

.rotate:hover {

transform: rotate(180deg);

}
```

Timing Functions

CSS transitions offer various timing functions to control the pace of the animation. The common timing functions include:

- ease: A smooth acceleration and deceleration (default).
- linear: A consistent speed throughout the transition.
- ease-in: Gradual acceleration.
- ease-out: Gradual deceleration.

- ease-in-out: Gradual acceleration and deceleration.

You can experiment with these timing functions to achieve the desired visual effect for your transitions.

In summary, CSS transitions are a powerful way to create smooth animations and interactions in web design without relying on JavaScript. By specifying the property, duration, timing function, and delay, you can control how elements transition between different states, adding a polished and engaging touch to your web projects.

Section 7.2: Keyframes and Animation Timings

While CSS transitions are excellent for simple animations, CSS animations offer more control and flexibility for complex and custom animations. In this section, we'll explore CSS animations, focusing on keyframes and animation timings.

Keyframes Animation

CSS animations are created using @keyframes rules. Keyframes allow you to define intermediate steps for an animation, specifying how an element should appear at different points during the animation.

Here's a basic structure for creating a keyframes animation:

/* Define keyframes for an animation */

@**keyframes** animationName {

0% {

/* Styles at the beginning of the animation (0% progress) */

}

50% {

/* Styles halfway through the animation (50% progress) */

}

100% {

/* Styles at the end of the animation (100% progress) */

}

}

You can name your animation (animationName in the example above) and specify different percentages (from 0% to 100%) to define the styles at various points during the animation.

Applying Keyframes Animation

To apply a keyframes animation to an element, you use the animation property. Here's the syntax for applying an animation:

/* Apply an animation to an element */

element {

animation: animationName duration timing-function delay iteration-count direction fill-mode play-state;

}

- animationName: The name of the animation defined with @keyframes.

- duration: The time it takes for the animation to complete (e.g., 1s for one second).

- timing-function: The acceleration curve for the animation (e.g., ease, linear, ease-in-out).

- delay: An optional delay before the animation starts (e.g., 0.2s for a 0.2-second delay).

- iteration-count: The number of times the animation repeats (e.g., infinite for infinite loops).

- direction: The direction of the animation (normal, reverse, alternate, alternate-reverse).

- fill-mode: Determines how the animation affects the element before and after it plays (forwards, backwards, both, none).

- play-state: Controls whether the animation is running or paused (running, paused).

Example of a Keyframes Animation

Let's create a simple keyframes animation that makes an element move from left to right:

```
/* Define a keyframes animation */

@keyframes slideRight {

0% {

transform: translateX(0);

}
```

```
100% {

transform: translateX(200px);

}

}

/* Apply the animation to an element */

.slide {

width: 100px;

height: 100px;

background-color: #3498db;

animation: slideRight 2s ease-in-out infinite alternate;

}
```

In this example, the .slide element will move horizontally from 0 to 200 pixels and back in an infinite loop with an ease-in-out timing function.

Animation Timing Functions and Delays

Just like with transitions, CSS animations can use various timing functions and delays to control the animation's pace and timing. You can experiment with different timing functions to achieve the desired animation effect.

```
/* Applying timing function and delay */

.element {
```

animation: animationName 2s cubic-bezier(0.68, -0.55, 0.27, 1.55) 0.5s infinite alternate;

}

Using Multiple Keyframes

Animations can include multiple keyframes, allowing you to create complex animations with precise control over each step. Combine keyframes to create animations that involve scaling, rotation, fading, and more.

/* Combining multiple keyframes for a complex animation */

@keyframes complexAnimation {

0% {

transform: scale(1);

opacity: 1;

}

50% {

transform: scale(1.2) rotate(45deg);

opacity: 0.5;

}

100% {

transform: scale(1) rotate(0deg);

opacity: 1;

}

```
}

.element {

    animation: complexAnimation 3s ease-in-out infinite;

}
```

Using Animation Events

You can also use JavaScript to listen for animation events like animationstart, animationend, and animationiteration to trigger actions or add interactivity to your animations.

In conclusion, CSS animations, especially when combined with keyframes, provide powerful tools for creating complex and custom animations on web elements. By defining keyframes and using animation properties, you can control the behavior, timing, and appearance of elements in your web projects, making them more engaging and interactive.

Section 7.3: Creating Smooth CSS Animations

In this section, we'll delve deeper into the world of CSS animations, focusing on techniques to create smooth and visually pleasing animations for your web projects. Smooth animations can greatly enhance the user experience by providing fluid transitions and engaging interactions.

Using transition-timing-function

One key aspect of creating smooth CSS animations is controlling the timing function. The transition-timing-function property allows you to define how the animation's speed varies over time. Here are some common timing functions:

- linear: Provides a constant speed throughout the animation, resulting in a linear motion.

- ease: Offers a smooth acceleration and deceleration, making animations appear more natural.

- ease-in: Starts slow and accelerates, creating a gentle beginning.

- ease-out: Slows down at the end, offering a gradual stop.

- ease-in-out: Combines ease-in and ease-out, creating a balanced animation.

You can experiment with different timing functions to achieve the desired animation effect. Here's an example of using transition-timing-function:

```
/* Applying different timing functions */
.element {

transition: transform 1s ease-in-out;

}

.element:hover {

transform: scale(1.2);

}
```

In this code, the element scales up smoothly with an ease-in-out timing function when hovered.

Handling Timing Delays

Smooth animations often involve precise timing. You can use the animation-delay property to introduce delays before animations start. This can be useful for creating staggered animations or synchronizing animations with other elements on the page.

```
/* Adding delays to animations */

.element {

animation: slideIn 1s ease-in-out 0.5s;

}

@keyframes slideIn {

from {

transform: translateX(-100%);

}

to {

transform: translateX(0);

}

}
```

In this example, the slideIn animation starts with a 0.5-second delay, creating a staggered entrance effect.

Using transform for Smooth Transitions

The transform property is often used to create smooth transitions and animations, especially for 2D and 3D transformations. You can use it for effects like scaling, rotating, translating, and skewing elements.

/ Using transform for smooth animations */*

.element {

transition: transform 0.5s ease-in-out;

}

.element:***hover*** {

transform: scale(1.2) rotate(45deg);

}

In this code, the element smoothly scales up and rotates when hovered, creating a visually pleasing animation.

Optimizing for Performance

While creating smooth animations is essential, it's also important to consider performance. Animations that are too complex or resource-intensive can lead to slow page load times and poor user experiences, especially on mobile devices.

Here are some tips for optimizing CSS animations:

- **Use GPU Acceleration**: Complex animations should be hardware-accelerated by the GPU for better performance. You can achieve this by using properties like transform and opacity.

- **Limit Animations**: Avoid overloading your page with too many animations. Focus on key elements and interactions to maintain performance.

- **Test on Various Devices**: Always test your animations on different devices and browsers to ensure they perform well everywhere.

- **Use CSS Hardware Acceleration**: Properties like will-change and transform can trigger GPU acceleration, improving animation smoothness.

- **Use RequestAnimationFrame**: For complex animations, consider using JavaScript with requestAnimationFrame for more precise control.

In summary, creating smooth CSS animations involves controlling timing functions, handling delays, and optimizing for performance. By paying attention to these aspects, you can enhance the user experience and make your web projects more engaging and visually appealing.

Section 7.4: Animation Effects for User Engagement

In this section, we'll explore various animation effects that you can use to enhance user engagement on your website or web application. Animations can be powerful tools for capturing user attention, providing feedback, and creating interactive user interfaces.

Hover Effects

One of the most common uses of animations for user engagement is implementing hover effects. These effects trigger when the user hovers their mouse pointer over an element. Hover animations can be used for buttons, links, images, and more to provide visual feedback and make interactive elements stand out.

```css
/* Creating a simple hover effect */

.button {

transition: transform 0.3s ease-in-out;

}

.button:hover {

transform: scale(1.1);

}
```

In this example, when the user hovers over a button with the class .button, it smoothly scales up, creating an engaging effect.

Click or Tap Animations

To make web interactions more engaging, you can apply animations to elements when they are clicked or tapped (on touch devices). This provides immediate feedback to the user, making interactions feel responsive.

```css
/* Adding a click animation */

.button {

transition: transform 0.2s ease-in-out;

}

.button:active {

transform: scale(0.9);

}
```

In this code, the button scales down slightly when clicked, giving the user feedback that their click has been recognized.

Loading Spinners

Loading spinners are commonly used to indicate that a process is in progress. They engage users by providing visual feedback that something is happening, which can reduce frustration during waiting times.

```
/* Creating a simple loading spinner */

.spinner {

border: 4px solid rgba(0, 0, 0, 0.1);

border-left: 4px solid #3498db;

animation: spin 1s linear infinite;

}

@keyframes spin {

0% {

transform: rotate(0deg);

}

100% {

transform: rotate(360deg);

}

}
```

In this example, the .spinner element displays a rotating animation using keyframes to indicate that a process is ongoing.

Scroll Animations

Scroll animations are a fantastic way to engage users as they explore your content. Elements can animate into view or change appearance as the user scrolls down the page.

```css
/* Scroll animation using CSS classes */

.animated {

opacity: 0;

transform: translateY(20px);

transition: opacity 0.5s ease, transform 0.5s ease;

}

.in-view {

opacity: 1;

transform: translateY(0);

}
```

In this code, elements with the class .animated start with reduced opacity and are translated downward. When they enter the viewport and gain the class .in-view, they smoothly transition to full opacity and their original position.

Modal Popups

Modal popups can engage users by displaying additional information or interactive content without leaving the current page. Animations can make these modals appear and disappear smoothly.

```css
/* Modal popup with animation */

.modal {

display: none;

position: fixed;

top: 0;

left: 0;

width: 100%;

height: 100%;

background: rgba(0, 0, 0, 0.7);

align-items: center;

justify-content: center;

}

.modal.active {

display: flex;

animation: fadeIn 0.3s ease;

}

@keyframes fadeIn {
```

```
from {

opacity: 0;

}

to {

opacity: 1;

}

}
```

In this example, the .modal is hidden by default but becomes visible with a fade-in animation when it gains the class .active.

Interactive Form Validation

Engage users in form interactions by providing real-time feedback through animations. For example, you can use animations to indicate valid or invalid form inputs.

```
/* Form input validation */

.input {

transition: border-color 0.3s ease;

}

.input.invalid {

border-color: #e74c3c;

animation: shake 0.3s ease;

}
```

```
@keyframes shake {

0%, 100% {

transform: translateX(0);

}

25%, 75% {

transform: translateX(-10px);

}

50% {

transform: translateX(10px);

}

}
```

In this code, when an input with the class .input is marked as invalid, it briefly shakes with the shake animation, drawing the user's attention to the issue.

These are just a few examples of how animations can enhance user engagement on your website or web application. By strategically using animations for feedback, interactivity, and visual appeal, you can create a more engaging and user-friendly experience.

Section 7.5: Performance Optimization for Animations

In this section, we'll explore performance optimization techniques for CSS animations. While animations can greatly enhance the user experience, they can also impact performance if not implemented carefully. By optimizing your animations, you can ensure that they run smoothly and do not negatively affect your website's speed and responsiveness.

Use Hardware Acceleration

One of the most effective ways to optimize CSS animations is to leverage hardware acceleration. When certain CSS properties like transform and opacity are used in animations, the browser can offload the animation calculations to the GPU (Graphics Processing Unit), resulting in smoother animations.

Here's an example:

/ Using transform for hardware-accelerated animations */*

.element {

transform: translate3d(0, 0, 0);

transition: transform 0.3s ease;

}

.element:*hover* {

transform: translate3d(20px, 0, 0);

}

By adding translate3d(0, 0, 0) to the transform property, you trigger hardware acceleration for the animation.

Optimize Animation Properties

To improve animation performance, focus on optimizing the properties you animate. Avoid animating properties that cause layout or paint recalculations, as these can be costly in terms of performance. Instead, prioritize properties that can be animated efficiently by the browser.

For example, animating transform and opacity is typically more efficient than animating width, height, or margin. When possible, use transform for complex animations.

Use requestAnimationFrame

For complex and synchronized animations, consider using JavaScript in conjunction with the requestAnimationFrame API. This API provides a smoother and more efficient way to schedule animations, especially when you need precise control over timing and synchronization.

```
function animateElement() {

const element = document.querySelector('.element');

let startTime;

function animate(timestamp) {

if (!startTime) startTime = timestamp;

const progress = (timestamp - startTime) / 1000; // Calculate animation progress

// Update element's state based on progress

element.style.transform = `translateX(${progress * 100}px)`;

if (progress < 1) {

requestAnimationFrame(animate); // Continue animation
```

```
}

}
```

requestAnimationFrame(animate); // *Start the animation*

```
}
```

By using requestAnimationFrame, you can ensure that animations are synchronized with the browser's rendering cycle, resulting in smoother performance.

Debounce and Throttle Animations

If you have animations triggered by user interactions like scrolling or resizing, consider debouncing or throttling those animations. Debouncing and throttling help prevent excessive animations from overloading the browser.

Debouncing involves delaying the animation until a certain time has passed since the last interaction, while throttling limits the animation frequency.

// *Debouncing scroll animations*

let debounceTimeout;

window.addEventListener('scroll', () => {

clearTimeout(debounceTimeout);

debounceTimeout = setTimeout(() => {

// *Perform animation when scrolling has stopped*

animateOnScroll();

}, 200); // *Adjust the debounce delay as needed*

});

By implementing debounce or throttle techniques, you can ensure that animations are triggered at an optimal rate, reducing performance bottlenecks.

Test and Measure Performance

Finally, always test and measure the performance of your animations on various devices and browsers. Tools like the browser's built-in DevTools can help you identify performance bottlenecks and optimize accordingly. Pay attention to metrics like FPS (Frames Per Second) and rendering times to ensure a smooth user experience.

In conclusion, optimizing CSS animations is crucial for maintaining a fast and responsive website. Use hardware acceleration, optimize animation properties, consider requestAnimationFrame, debounce or throttle animations, and continuously test and measure performance to ensure that your animations enhance the user experience without sacrificing speed and responsiveness.

Chapter 8: Styling Forms and User Interfaces

Section 8.1: Customizing Form Elements

In this section, we'll delve into the art of customizing form elements using CSS. Forms are an essential part of web applications, and customizing their appearance not only improves aesthetics but also enhances the user experience.

Basic Form Styling

Customizing form elements like input fields, checkboxes, and radio buttons is achieved through CSS. You can use CSS properties like border, background, padding, and color to style these elements according to your design.

/* Example of styling input fields */

input[type="text"],

input[type="email"] {

width: 100%;

padding: 10px;

border: 1px solid #ccc;

border-radius: 5px;

font-size: 16px;

}

/* Styling checkboxes and radio buttons */

```
input[type="checkbox"],

input[type="radio"] {

margin-right: 5px;

}
```

In this example, we set the width, padding, border, and font size for text and email input fields, and we adjust the margin for checkboxes and radio buttons.

Placeholder Text

You can style the placeholder text within input fields using the ::placeholder pseudo-element. This allows you to change its color, font size, and other properties.

```
/* Styling placeholder text */

input::placeholder {

color: #999;

font-size: 14px;

}
```

Focus and Hover Styles

It's essential to provide visual feedback when users interact with form elements. You can use :focus and :hover pseudo-classes to define styles for these states.

```
/* Styling for focused input fields */

input:focus {
```

border-color: #007bff;

box-shadow: 0 0 5px rgba(0, 123, 255, 0.5);

}

/* Styling for hover effect */

button:*hover* {

background-color: #007bff;

color: #fff;

}

In this code, input fields receive a blue border and a subtle box shadow when focused, and buttons change background and text color on hover.

Custom Buttons

Buttons are an integral part of forms and user interfaces. You can create custom buttons by defining their appearance, including background, border, padding, and text color.

/* Styling custom buttons */

button {

background-color: #007bff;

color: #fff;

border: none;

padding: 10px 20px;

cursor: pointer;

border-radius: 5px;

}

/* *Button hover effect* */

button:***hover*** {

background-color: #0056b3;

}

Here, we style buttons with a blue background, white text, and some padding. On hover, the background color changes to a slightly darker shade.

Form Validation Styles

When implementing form validation, it's helpful to provide visual cues to users. You can style valid and invalid input fields differently using the :valid and :invalid pseudo-classes.

/* *Styling valid and invalid input fields* */

input:***valid*** {

border-color: #4caf50; /* *Green border for valid input* */

}

input:***invalid*** {

border-color: #f44336; /* *Red border for invalid input* */

}

These styles help users understand whether their input meets the required criteria.

Customizing Select Boxes

Select boxes (dropdowns) can also be customized to match your design. You can style the background, border, arrow icon, and more.

```css
/* Styling custom select boxes */

select {

appearance: none; /* Remove default arrow icon */

background-color: #fff;

border: 1px solid #ccc;

padding: 10px;

border-radius: 5px;

}

/* Adding a custom arrow icon */

select::after {

content: "\25BC"; /* Downward arrow character */

position: absolute;

top: 50%;

right: 10px;

transform: translateY(-50%);

}
```

In this example, we remove the default arrow icon, style the select box, and add a custom arrow using the ::after pseudo-element.

Customizing form elements with CSS not only enhances the visual appeal of your web forms but also improves user interaction. By applying these CSS techniques, you can create user-friendly and aesthetically pleasing forms and user interfaces.

Section 8.2: Creating Stylish Buttons and Inputs

In this section, we'll explore advanced techniques for creating stylish buttons and input elements using CSS. Customizing these elements can greatly enhance the visual appeal of your website and improve the user experience.

Creating Gradient Buttons

One popular way to style buttons is by using gradients. Gradients create a smooth transition between colors, giving buttons a modern and appealing look. You can use the background-image property with gradient values to achieve this effect.

/ Stylish gradient button */*

.button-gradient {

background-image: linear-gradient(to bottom, #3498db, #2980b9);

color: #fff;

padding: 10px 20px;

border: none;

border-radius: 5px;

cursor: pointer;

```
}
```

/* Hover effect for the gradient button */

```
.button-gradient:hover {

background-image: linear-gradient(to bottom, #2980b9, #3498db);

}
```

In this example, we create a button with a gradient background that transitions from a light blue to a darker blue. The button's appearance changes on hover to provide visual feedback to users.

Styling Rounded and Circular Buttons

Rounded and circular buttons are trendy and can add a touch of elegance to your design. You can achieve this by setting a border-radius property to control the curvature of the button.

/* Rounded button */

```
.button-rounded {

background-color: #f39c12;

color: #fff;

padding: 10px 20px;

border-radius: 25px; /* Adjust the value to control the roundness */

cursor: pointer;

}
```

/* Circular button */

```css
.button-circular {

background-color: #e74c3c;

color: #fff;

width: 50px; /* Ensure width and height are equal for a perfect circle */

height: 50px;

border-radius: 50%; /* Makes the button circular */

cursor: pointer;

}
```

Here, we create a rounded button with a specified border-radius, and a circular button by setting border-radius to 50% and ensuring equal width and height.

Adding Icons to Buttons

Icons can make buttons more visually engaging and convey meaning. You can include icons by using web fonts, inline SVG, or background images.

```css
/* Button with a FontAwesome icon */

.button-icon {

background-color: #2ecc71;

color: #fff;

padding: 10px 20px;

border-radius: 5px;
```

```
cursor: pointer;

}

/* Styling the FontAwesome icon */

.button-icon i {

margin-right: 5px;

}

/* Button with an inline SVG icon */

.button-svg {

background-color: #9b59b6;

color: #fff;

padding: 10px 20px;

border-radius: 5px;

cursor: pointer;

background-image:                url('data:image/svg+xml;utf8,<svg
xmlns="http://www.w3.org/2000/svg"                width="16"
height="16"><circle cx="8" cy="8" r="7" fill="%23ffffff"/><path
d="M7 4v8l7-4z" fill="%23ffffff"/></svg>');

background-repeat: no-repeat;

background-position: right center;

}

/* Button with a background image icon */
```

```css
.button-bg-icon {

background-color: #f1c40f;

color: #fff;

padding: 10px 20px;

border-radius: 5px;

cursor: pointer;

background-image: url('icon.png');

background-repeat: no-repeat;

background-position: left center;

padding-left: 40px; /* Adjust to match the icon width */

}
```

In these examples, we demonstrate adding FontAwesome icons, inline SVG icons, and background image icons to buttons. Adjust the styles and icons as needed for your design.

Custom Input Focus Styles

Styling the focus state of input fields is crucial for improving accessibility and user experience. You can customize the focus styles by changing properties like border-color and box-shadow.

```css
/* Custom focus styles for input fields */

.input-focus {

border: 2px solid #3498db;

box-shadow: 0 0 5px rgba(52, 152, 219, 0.5);
```

}

By defining custom focus styles, you can make it clear which input field is currently active and enhance usability.

These advanced techniques for styling buttons and input elements will help you create visually appealing and user-friendly forms and interfaces. Experiment with these styles to achieve the desired look and feel for your website or web application.

Section 8.3: CSS for Dropdowns and Select Boxes

Dropdown menus and select boxes are common elements in web forms and user interfaces. In this section, we'll explore how to style and customize these components using CSS to create a more engaging and user-friendly experience.

Styling Dropdown Menus

Dropdown menus often consist of an outer container and a list of options. You can style both the container and the options to match your design.

/* Style the dropdown container */

.dropdown {

position: relative;

display: inline-block;

border: 1px solid #ccc;

border-radius: 4px;

background-color: #fff;

padding: 5px;

cursor: pointer;

}

/ Style the dropdown options */*

.dropdown-options {

display: none;

position: absolute;

background-color: #fff;

border: 1px solid #ccc;

border-radius: 4px;

box-shadow: 0 2px 5px rgba(0, 0, 0, 0.2);

z-index: 1;

}

/ Show the dropdown options on hover or focus */*

.dropdown:***hover*** .dropdown-options,

.dropdown:***focus*** .dropdown-options {

display: block;

}

In this example, we create a dropdown container and style it with rounded corners, a border, and a hover/focus effect to reveal the options. The options are hidden by default but displayed when the container is hovered over or receives focus.

Customizing Select Boxes

Select boxes, also known as dropdown select lists, can be customized to match your design theme.

/* Style the select box */

.select-box {

appearance: none; /* Hide the default dropdown arrow */

padding: 8px;

border: 1px solid #ccc;

border-radius: 4px;

background-color: #fff;

cursor: pointer;

}

/* Style the select box on hover or focus */

.select-box:*hover*,

.select-box:*focus* {

border-color: #3498db;

}

/* Style the dropdown arrow */

.select-box::*after* {

content: "\25BC"; /* *Unicode arrow character* */

position: absolute;

top: 50%;

right: 10px;

transform: translateY(-50%);

}

In this code, we hide the default browser appearance of the select box and replace it with a custom design. We also style the dropdown arrow using a Unicode arrow character.

Creating Custom Dropdown Icons

To further enhance the visual appeal of dropdown menus, you can add custom icons next to the selected option.

/* *Style the custom dropdown icon* */

.custom-dropdown-icon**::after** {

content: "\25BC"; /* *Unicode arrow character* */

position: absolute;

top: 50%;

right: 10px;

transform: translateY(-50%);

}

/* *Apply the custom icon to a specific select box* */

```css
.custom-dropdown .select-box::after {

content: "\25BA"; /* Unicode right arrow character */

}
```

In this code, we define a custom dropdown icon and apply it to a specific select box with the class .custom-dropdown. You can replace the content of the ::after pseudo-element with different Unicode characters or custom icons.

Styling dropdowns and select boxes allows you to create a cohesive design for your forms and user interfaces, enhancing the overall user experience on your website or web application. Experiment with these styles to achieve the desired look and feel for your project.

Section 8.4: Styling Radio Buttons and Checkboxes

In this section, we'll delve into the customization of radio buttons and checkboxes using CSS. These form elements are essential for user input and can benefit from visual enhancements that match your website's design.

Customizing Radio Buttons

Radio buttons are often used when users need to select a single option from a list. You can style them to make them more visually appealing and in line with your design.

```css
/* Hide the default radio button */

.radio-button {

appearance: none;
```

```
-webkit-appearance: none;

-moz-appearance: none;

width: 16px;

height: 16px;

border: 1px solid #ccc;

border-radius: 50%;

background-color: #fff;

cursor: pointer;

margin-right: 8px;

}

/* Style the radio button when selected */

.radio-button:checked {

background-color: #3498db; /* Change the background color */

border: 1px solid #3498db;

}
```

In this code, we hide the default appearance of radio buttons and create custom styles. When a radio button is selected (checked), its background color and border change, providing visual feedback to users.

Styling Checkboxes

Checkboxes are used when users need to make multiple selections from a list. Similar to radio buttons, you can style checkboxes to match your design.

/ Hide the default checkbox */*

.checkbox {

appearance: none;

-webkit-appearance: none;

-moz-appearance: none;

width: 16px;

height: 16px;

border: 1px solid #ccc;

background-color: #fff;

cursor: pointer;

margin-right: 8px;

}

/ Style the checkbox when checked */*

.checkbox*:checked* {

background-color: #3498db; */* Change the background color */*

border: 1px solid #3498db;

}

```
/* Style the checkbox label */

.checkbox-label {

cursor: pointer;

}
```

This code hides the default appearance of checkboxes and provides custom styling. When a checkbox is checked, its background color and border change. Additionally, we've added styles to make the label clickable for a better user experience.

Creating Custom Icons for Checkboxes

To make your checkboxes more unique, you can replace the default checkbox icon with custom icons using pseudo-elements.

```
/* Style the custom checkbox icon */

.custom-checkbox::before {

content: "\2713"; /* Unicode checkmark character */

font-size: 16px;

line-height: 16px;

color: #fff;

position: absolute;

top: 0;

left: 0;

opacity: 0;

}
```

/* Style the checkbox when checked */

.custom-checkbox***:checked::before*** {

opacity: 1;

}

In this code, we use the ::before pseudo-element to insert a checkmark icon before the checkbox. The icon becomes visible when the checkbox is checked, providing a visual indication of the selection.

Customizing radio buttons and checkboxes not only improves their appearance but also enhances user interaction. Users are more likely to engage with stylish and intuitive form elements, contributing to a better user experience on your website or web application.

Section 8.5: Validation and Error Messages

In web forms, validation is a crucial aspect of ensuring that users provide accurate and complete information. Additionally, providing clear error messages when validation fails is essential for a positive user experience. In this section, we'll explore how to style and customize validation and error messages using CSS.

Styling Validation States

HTML5 introduced built-in form validation states, such as :valid and :invalid, that you can style with CSS. These states allow you to apply specific styles to valid and invalid form elements.

/* Style valid form controls */

input***:valid***,

textarea:*valid*,

select:*valid* {

border: 1px solid #2ecc71; /* *Green border for valid input* */

}

/* *Style invalid form controls* */

input:*invalid*,

textarea:*invalid*,

select:*invalid* {

border: 1px solid #e74c3c; /* *Red border for invalid input* */

}

In this example, valid inputs have a green border, while invalid inputs have a red border. This visual feedback helps users understand whether their input is correct.

Customizing Error Messages

When a user submits a form with invalid input, it's essential to provide clear error messages. You can style these error messages to make them more noticeable and user-friendly.

/* *Style the error message container* */

.error-message {

color: #e74c3c; /* *Red text color for error messages* */

font-size: 14px;

margin-top: 5px;

display: none;

}

/* *Display the error message when the input is invalid* */

input:*invalid* + .error-message,

textarea:*invalid* + .error-message,

select:*invalid* + .error-message {

display: block;

}

In this code, we style the error message container with red text and hide it by default using display: none. When an input is invalid, the adjacent error message with the class .error-message is displayed, making the error apparent to the user.

Customizing Validation Styles for Different Inputs

You can further customize the appearance of valid and invalid inputs by targeting specific input types or attributes.

/* *Style valid and invalid email inputs* */

input[type="email"]:*valid*,

input[type="email"]:*invalid* {

border: 1px solid #3498db;

}

/* *Style valid and invalid required inputs* */

input[required]:*valid*,

input[required]:*invalid* {

border: 1px solid #e74c3c;

}

In this example, we apply styles to email inputs and required inputs differently, ensuring that the visual feedback matches the input type.

Enhancing Accessibility

Remember to ensure that your validation and error message styles are accessible. Consider using ARIA roles and attributes to provide additional information to assistive technologies and users with disabilities.

By customizing validation and error message styles, you can guide users through the form-filling process more effectively and improve the overall usability of your web forms. These visual cues help users understand what's expected and how to correct any errors they encounter.

Chapter 9: Responsive Web Design Techniques

Section 9.1: Introduction to Responsive Web Design

Responsive web design is an essential approach in modern web development. It focuses on creating web pages that adapt and look great on various devices and screen sizes, including desktops, tablets, and smartphones. In this section, we'll introduce the concept of responsive web design and discuss its importance.

The Need for Responsive Design

The rise of mobile devices has changed the way people access the internet. Websites need to be accessible and user-friendly across a wide range of screen sizes and orientations. Here are some key reasons why responsive design is crucial:

1. **Multi-Device Compatibility:** Users may access your website from different devices, and responsive design ensures a consistent experience.
2. **Improved User Experience:** Responsive sites adapt to the user's screen, making navigation and content consumption more comfortable.
3. **SEO Benefits:** Search engines favor mobile-friendly websites, which can positively impact your search rankings.
4. **Cost-Efficiency:** Building a responsive site is often more cost-effective than maintaining separate desktop and mobile versions.

Principles of Responsive Design

Responsive design is built on several core principles:

1. Fluid Grids

Instead of fixed-width layouts, responsive designs use fluid grids that adapt to the screen size. This allows content to flow and reorganize as needed.

.container {

width: 100%;

max-width: 1200px; /* *Set a maximum width for large screens* */

margin: 0 auto; /* *Center the container* */

}

2. Flexible Images

Images should also resize with the layout. You can use CSS to ensure that images don't exceed their container's width.

img {

max-width: 100%;

height: auto; /* *Maintain aspect ratio* */

}

3. Media Queries

Media queries are CSS rules that apply based on the screen's characteristics, such as width, height, and orientation. They allow you to create different layouts for different devices.

@media (**max-width**: 768px) {

/* Styles for screens smaller than 768px wide */

}

4. Mobile-First Approach

Starting with a mobile-friendly design and then enhancing it for larger screens is known as the mobile-first approach. It ensures that your site is optimized for smaller screens first.

5. Content Priority

Consider the most critical content and make sure it's prominently displayed, especially on smaller screens where space is limited.

Responsive web design is an ongoing process that involves testing and refining your layouts on various devices. It's a skill that every web developer should master to create websites that provide an optimal experience for all users, regardless of their device. In the following sections, we'll explore specific techniques and tools for achieving responsive design.

Section 9.2: Media Queries for Different Screen Sizes

Media queries are a fundamental tool in responsive web design. They allow you to apply specific CSS styles based on the characteristics of the user's device, such as screen width, height, and orientation. In this section, we'll explore how to use media queries to create responsive designs for various screen sizes.

Syntax of Media Queries

Media queries use the @media rule in CSS and follow a specific syntax. Here's a basic example:

@media (**max-width**: 768px) {

/* Styles for screens with a maximum width of 768px */

body {

font-size: 16px;

}

}

In this example, the styles inside the media query block will apply when the screen's width is 768 pixels or less. You can also use min-width to target larger screens:

@media (**min-width**: 1024px) {

/* Styles for screens with a minimum width of 1024px */

body {

font-size: 18px;

```
}

}
```

Common Media Query Breakpoints

Choosing the right breakpoints for your media queries is crucial to create a responsive design that works well across a range of devices. While the specific breakpoints depend on your design and content, here are some common ones:

- **Extra Small (Phones):** @media (max-width: 576px)

- **Small (Tablets):** @media (min-width: 576px)

- **Medium (Laptops):** @media (min-width: 768px)

- **Large (Desktops):** @media (min-width: 992px)

- **Extra Large (Large Desktops):** @media (min-width: 1200px)

These breakpoints cover a wide range of devices, from small smartphones to large desktop screens.

Applying Different Styles

Media queries allow you to apply different styles at different screen sizes. For example, you can change font sizes, margins, or even completely reorganize your layout:

@media (max-width: 768px) {

/ Styles for smaller screens */*

header {

```css
font-size: 24px;

}

nav {

display: none; /* Hide navigation on small screens */

}

}

@media (min-width: 768px) {

/* Styles for larger screens */

header {

font-size: 32px;

}

nav {

display: block; /* Show navigation on larger screens */

}

}
```

By adjusting styles based on screen size, you can create a seamless and user-friendly experience for your website's visitors.

Mobile-First Approach

A common approach in responsive design is to start with mobile styles and then enhance the design for larger screens. This approach ensures that your site looks good on small screens and progressively improves on larger ones. To implement a mobile-first approach, you reverse the logic of your media queries:

/* Default styles for all screens */

body {

font-size: 16px;

}

/* Styles for screens larger than 768px */

@media (**min-width**: 768px) {

body {

font-size: 18px;

}

}

This mobile-first approach is considered a best practice in responsive design.

Media queries are a powerful tool for creating responsive web designs that adapt to various screen sizes and devices. They allow you to fine-tune your styles to provide the best possible user experience on different platforms. In the next section, we'll explore fluid layouts and flexible images, which are essential components of responsive design.

Section 9.3: Fluid Layouts and Flexible Images

Creating responsive web designs involves more than just adjusting styles with media queries. It also requires designing layouts and images to be flexible and fluid, ensuring that they adapt gracefully to different screen sizes. In this section, we'll delve into the concepts of fluid layouts and flexible images.

Fluid Layouts

A fluid layout is one that adapts to the width of the user's screen, expanding or contracting as needed. Unlike fixed-width layouts, which have a static width, fluid layouts are defined in relative units like percentages. Here's how you can create a simple fluid layout:

.container {

width: 90%; /* *Use a percentage for the container's width* */

max-width: 1200px; /* *Set a maximum width to avoid overly wide layouts* */

margin: 0 auto; /* *Center the container horizontally* */

}

In this example, the .container element takes up 90% of its parent's width but never exceeds 1200 pixels. This approach ensures that the layout scales smoothly on various screens.

Flexible Images

Images are a crucial part of web content, and they, too, need to adapt to different screen sizes. To make images flexible, use the following CSS:

```
img {
```

max-width: 100%; /* *Ensure images never exceed their container's width* */

height: auto; /* *Maintain the aspect ratio of the image* */

```
}
```

By setting max-width to 100%, you ensure that images scale down when their container's width decreases but maintain their aspect ratio to prevent distortion.

Combining Fluid Layouts and Flexible Images

To create a truly responsive design, combine fluid layouts and flexible images with media queries. Here's an example that adjusts both the layout and images based on screen width:

/* *Default styles for all screens* */

```
.container {
```

width: 90%;

max-width: 1200px;

margin: 0 auto;

```
}
```

```
img {
```

max-width: 100%;

height: auto;

```
}
```

```
/* Styles for screens larger than 768px */

@media (min-width: 768px) {

.container {

width: 80%; /* Adjust container width for larger screens */

}

img {

/* Increase image size on larger screens if needed */

}

}
```

By using relative units and flexible image styles within media queries, you can ensure that your website's layout and images adapt gracefully to various devices.

Testing and Fine-Tuning

Responsive design involves testing your site on different devices and screen sizes to identify any issues and make necessary adjustments. Browser developer tools and online testing tools can be valuable resources for this process. Additionally, real user testing on various devices is invaluable for ensuring a smooth user experience.

In the next section, we'll explore the mobile-first approach to responsive design and discuss its benefits.

Section 9.4: Mobile-First and Desktop-First Approaches

When developing responsive web designs, one important consideration is the approach you take: mobile-first or desktop-first. These approaches dictate how you build your CSS styles and media queries to cater to different screen sizes.

Mobile-First Approach

The mobile-first approach prioritizes designing and coding for small screens (e.g., mobile phones) first and then progressively enhancing the design for larger screens. This approach has gained popularity because it encourages simplicity, performance, and a better user experience for mobile users.

To implement the mobile-first approach, you start with your base styles for small screens and use media queries to add styles for larger screens. Here's a basic example:

```css
/* Base styles for small screens */

body {

font-size: 16px;

}

/* Media query for screens larger than 768px (tablets and desktops) */

@media (min-width: 768px) {

body {

font-size: 18px;

}
```

```
}
```

In this example, the base font size is set for small screens, and a media query adjusts it for screens wider than 768px. This ensures a better reading experience on larger devices.

Desktop-First Approach

The desktop-first approach, as the name suggests, begins with designing and coding for larger screens (e.g., desktops) and then scaling down for smaller screens. While this approach is less common today, it can still be useful for projects where desktop users have more demanding requirements.

To implement the desktop-first approach, you start with your base styles for large screens and use media queries to make adjustments for smaller screens. Here's an example:

```css
/* Base styles for large screens */

body {

font-size: 18px;

}

/* Media query for screens smaller than 768px (tablets and mobiles) */

@media (max-width: 767px) {

body {

font-size: 16px;

}

}
```

In this example, the base font size is set for large screens, and a media query reduces it for screens narrower than 768px.

Choosing the Right Approach

The choice between mobile-first and desktop-first depends on your project's goals and audience. Mobile-first is generally recommended for most web projects because it promotes a user-centric approach, emphasizing simplicity and performance. It also aligns with Google's mobile-first indexing, which considers mobile content as the primary source for ranking.

However, for specialized applications or websites with a predominantly desktop audience, the desktop-first approach may be more suitable. It allows you to optimize the experience for desktop users and progressively enhance it for smaller screens.

In practice, many designers and developers prefer the mobile-first approach due to its user-centered focus and compatibility with modern web practices. Whichever approach you choose, the key is to create responsive designs that deliver a seamless experience across all devices.

In the following section, we'll explore techniques for testing and debugging responsive designs to ensure they work flawlessly on various screens.

Section 9.5: Testing and Debugging Responsiveness

Creating responsive web designs is a multi-faceted task, and it's essential to thoroughly test and debug your designs to ensure they work as intended on various devices and screen sizes. In this section, we'll explore the importance of testing and debugging responsiveness and discuss some effective techniques.

The Importance of Testing Responsiveness

Responsive web design aims to provide an optimal user experience across a wide range of devices, from smartphones and tablets to desktop computers. Testing responsiveness is crucial because it helps identify and resolve issues that may arise on different screens, browsers, and operating systems.

Without proper testing, users may encounter problems such as:

- Content not fitting on the screen.

- Elements overlapping or misaligned.

- Images not scaling correctly.

- Navigation menus becoming unusable.

- Slow loading times on mobile devices.

To avoid these issues and ensure a consistent and user-friendly experience, testing is essential.

Testing Methods and Tools

1. **Browser Developer Tools**: Most modern web browsers come with built-in developer tools that allow you to simulate different device sizes and screen orientations. You can use these tools to preview your website's responsiveness and debug issues in real-time.

2. **Online Responsive Testing Tools**: Several online tools provide a convenient way to test your website on various

devices and screen sizes. Tools like BrowserStack, Responsinator, and CrossBrowserTesting allow you to see how your site behaves on different platforms without having access to physical devices.

3. **Physical Devices**: Whenever possible, test your website on actual mobile devices, tablets, and various desktop monitors. This provides the most accurate representation of how users will experience your site.

4. **Emulators and Simulators**: Emulators and simulators are software tools that mimic the behavior of different devices and screen sizes. These tools are particularly useful for testing on older or less common devices that you may not have access to.

Key Areas to Test

When testing responsiveness, pay attention to the following key areas:

- **Layout**: Ensure that your layout adjusts correctly to different screen sizes. Test both portrait and landscape orientations on mobile devices.

- **Typography**: Check that your text remains readable and doesn't overflow or become too small on small screens.

- **Images and Media**: Verify that images scale appropriately, and media elements like videos and audio players function as expected on all devices.

- **Navigation**: Test your website's navigation menus and buttons to ensure they are accessible and user-friendly on touchscreens.

- **Forms**: Confirm that form fields and buttons are easily clickable and that input validation works as intended on mobile devices.

User Testing

While automated testing tools and emulators are valuable, nothing beats real user testing. Encourage users with different devices and screen sizes to visit your website and provide feedback. This can help you discover issues that may not be apparent through automated testing.

In conclusion, testing and debugging responsiveness are critical steps in the web design process. By thoroughly evaluating your website on various devices and using appropriate testing methods and tools, you can deliver a seamless and user-friendly experience to your audience, regardless of the device they use.

Chapter 10: CSS Preprocessors and Postprocessors

Section 10.1: What Are CSS Preprocessors?

CSS preprocessors are powerful tools that enhance the capabilities of traditional CSS (Cascading Style Sheets). They introduce programming features into the styling process, allowing developers to write more efficient and maintainable CSS code. In this section, we will delve into what CSS preprocessors are, why they are useful, and some popular options.

What Is a CSS Preprocessor?

A CSS preprocessor is a scripting language that extends the CSS syntax, allowing you to write CSS code in a more structured and dynamic way. Preprocessors introduce features like variables, nesting, functions, and mixins that are not available in standard CSS. These features make it easier to write and manage complex stylesheets.

Key Features of CSS Preprocessors:

1. **Variables**: Preprocessors allow you to define variables to store values such as colors, fonts, or sizes. This makes it easy to maintain consistency throughout your stylesheets.

$primary-color: #3498db;

body {

background-color: $primary-color;

}

1. **Nesting**: Preprocessors enable you to nest CSS rules within one another, making the code more organized and readable.

.container {

width: 100%;

.inner {

margin: 10px;

}

}

1. **Functions and Operations**: You can use functions and mathematical operations to calculate values dynamically. This is particularly useful for responsive designs.

$base-font-size: 16px;

.text-large {

font-size: $base-font-size * 1.25;

}

1. **Mixins**: Mixins allow you to define reusable blocks of CSS code that can be included in multiple places. This promotes code reusability and reduces duplication.

@**mixin** border-radius($radius) {

border-radius: $radius;

}

```
.button {

@include border-radius(5px);

}
```

1. **Importing**: Preprocessors support splitting your styles into multiple files and then importing them into a single stylesheet, making your codebase more modular and manageable.

```
@import 'variables';

@import 'layout';
```

Popular CSS Preprocessors:

1. **Sass (Syntactically Awesome Style Sheets)**: Sass is one of the most widely used CSS preprocessors. It comes in two syntax flavors: Sass (indented) and SCSS (Sassy CSS). Sass provides all the features mentioned above.
2. **Less**: Less is similar to Sass and offers features like variables, nesting, and mixins. It uses a JavaScript engine for compilation.
3. **Stylus**: Stylus is known for its concise and expressive syntax. It includes variables, mixins, and functions, and it's written in JavaScript.
4. **PostCSS**: While not a preprocessor in the traditional sense, PostCSS is a tool for transforming CSS with JavaScript. It can be configured to work with various plugins, effectively allowing you to create a custom preprocessor.

Why Use CSS Preprocessors?

CSS preprocessors offer several advantages:

- **Code Reusability**: You can create reusable styles and components with mixins and functions, reducing code duplication.

- **Maintainability**: Variables and nesting make your code more organized and easier to maintain.

- **Efficiency**: Preprocessors allow you to write cleaner and more efficient CSS code.

- **Compatibility**: Preprocessor files can be compiled into standard CSS, ensuring compatibility with all browsers.

- **Community and Ecosystem**: Preprocessors like Sass have large communities and libraries that provide useful tools and resources.

In summary, CSS preprocessors are valuable tools for web developers, providing a more efficient and maintainable way to write CSS. They enhance CSS with features like variables, nesting, and mixins, making it easier to create and manage complex stylesheets. The choice of which preprocessor to use depends on your preferences and project requirements.

Section 10.2: Working with SASS and SCSS

Sass (Syntactically Awesome Style Sheets) and SCSS (Sassy CSS) are two syntax options for the Sass preprocessor. In this section, we will explore the features and usage of both Sass and SCSS, highlighting their differences and similarities.

Sass (Indented Syntax)

Sass, often referred to as the "indented syntax," uses indentation and a minimalistic approach to writing styles. It omits braces and semicolons, relying on proper indentation to define code blocks.

Here's a basic example of Sass syntax:

$primary-color: #3498db

body

background-color: $primary-color

.container

width: 100%

.inner

margin: 10px

Key points about Sass (indented syntax):

- Uses indentation instead of curly braces.
- No semicolons are needed to separate style rules.
- Variable declaration starts with a $ sign.
- It has a more concise and clean look compared to CSS.

SCSS (Sassy CSS)

SCSS, on the other hand, is an extension of CSS and closely resembles traditional CSS syntax. It uses curly braces and semicolons, making it more familiar to developers who are already comfortable with CSS.

Here's the same example in SCSS syntax:

```
$primary-color: #3498db;

body {

background-color: $primary-color;

}

.container {

width: 100%;

.inner {

margin: 10px;

}

}
```

Key points about SCSS:

- Resembles CSS syntax with curly braces and semicolons.

- Variable declaration starts with a $ sign, just like in Sass.

- Provides a smooth transition for developers already familiar with CSS.

Choosing Between Sass and SCSS

The choice between Sass and SCSS often comes down to personal preference and project requirements. Here are some considerations:

- **Sass (Indented Syntax):**

– Offers a more concise and clean syntax.

– Requires careful attention to indentation.

– May be preferred by developers who like a minimalistic approach.

• **SCSS (Sassy CSS):**

– Resembles standard CSS, making it easier for CSS developers to transition.

– Uses familiar curly braces and semicolons.

– Tends to be the more popular choice in the Sass ecosystem.

Both Sass and SCSS provide the same powerful features, including variables, nesting, mixins, and functions. The choice between them won't significantly impact the capabilities of the preprocessor. It's essential to choose the syntax that you and your team are most comfortable with.

Using Sass and SCSS in Your Workflow

To use Sass or SCSS in your development workflow, you'll need to compile them into standard CSS before deploying your web application. Various tools and build systems can perform this compilation step. Some popular options include:

• **Command-Line Sass**: You can use the command-line Sass compiler to manually compile your Sass or SCSS files into CSS.

- **Task Runners**: Build tools like Gulp and Grunt can automate the compilation process. You can set up tasks to watch for changes in your Sass/SCSS files and compile them on the fly.

- **Webpack**: If you're using Webpack as your build system, there are loaders available that can compile Sass and SCSS as part of your build process.

- **Integrated Development Environments (IDEs)**: Many code editors and IDEs have extensions or built-in support for Sass and SCSS compilation.

Remember to include the necessary build step in your project to ensure that your Sass or SCSS styles are converted into CSS that browsers can understand.

In summary, Sass and SCSS are powerful CSS preprocessors that enhance the way you write stylesheets. While Sass uses indentation for a minimalistic approach, SCSS closely resembles standard CSS syntax with curly braces and semicolons. The choice between them is a matter of personal preference, and both offer the same features and capabilities. To use Sass or SCSS in your projects, you'll need to compile them into CSS using various build tools or IDE integrations.

Section 10.3: LESS and Stylus: Alternatives to SASS

In addition to Sass and SCSS, there are two other popular CSS preprocessors: LESS and Stylus. In this section, we'll explore LESS and Stylus as alternatives to Sass and SCSS, discussing their features, syntax, and use cases.

LESS

LESS is a CSS preprocessor that stands for "Leaner Style Sheets." It was created to simplify and improve CSS development. Here are some key features and syntax elements of LESS:

- **Variables**: Similar to Sass, LESS allows you to define variables to store reusable values.

@primary-color: #3498db;

body {

background-color: @primary-color;

}

- **Mixins**: LESS supports mixins, which are reusable blocks of styles that can be included in other selectors.

.border-radius(@radius) {

border-radius: @radius;

}

.button {

.border-radius(4px);

}

- **Nesting**: You can nest selectors inside other selectors to create a hierarchical structure, making your code more organized.

.navbar {

```
ul {

list-style: none;

}

}
```

- **Functions**: LESS provides built-in functions for performing various operations, such as color manipulation.

```
@base-color: #3498db;

@lighter-color: lighten(@base-color, 10%);
```

- **Importing**: You can split your styles into multiple LESS files and import them into your main file.

```
@import "variables.less";

@import "buttons.less";
```

LESS is known for its simplicity and ease of learning. It's a good choice if you want a CSS preprocessor that's lightweight and straightforward.

Stylus

Stylus is another CSS preprocessor that aims to provide a more expressive and flexible syntax. Here are some features and syntax elements of Stylus:

- **No Braces or Semicolons**: Stylus uses indentation instead of braces and semicolons, resulting in a cleaner and more concise syntax.

```
primary-color = #3498db

body

background-color primary-color
```

- **Variables and Mixins**: Stylus supports variables and mixins, similar to LESS and Sass.

```
primary-color = #3498db

button

background-color primary-color

border-radius(radius)

border-radius radius
```

- **Nesting**: Like Sass, Stylus allows for nesting of selectors.

```
.navbar

ul

list-style none
```

- **Mathematical Operations**: Stylus allows you to perform mathematical operations directly in your styles.

```
font-size = 16px

line-height = 1.5

padding = font-size * line-height
```

- **Importing**: You can split your Stylus code into separate files and import them as needed.

```
@import "variables.styl"
```

```
@import "buttons.styl"
```

Stylus is known for its flexibility and expressive syntax. It's an excellent choice for developers who prefer a more concise and less verbose way of writing styles.

Choosing Between LESS, Stylus, and Sass/SCSS

The choice between LESS, Stylus, and Sass/SCSS depends on your personal preference and project requirements. Here are some considerations:

- **LESS:**

  – Simple and easy to learn.

  – Syntax is closer to traditional CSS.

  – Good choice for those transitioning from standard CSS.

- **Stylus:**

  – Offers an extremely concise and expressive syntax.

  – Indentation-based, which some developers find more natural.

  – Suitable for projects where code readability and brevity are crucial.

- **Sass/SCSS:**

  – Widely adopted and supported in the industry.

  – Provides a balance between readability and power.

– Ideal for larger projects with complex styles.

Each of these preprocessors has its strengths, and your choice should align with your team's familiarity and the specific needs of your project. Regardless of the preprocessor you choose, they all enhance CSS development by introducing features like variables, mixins, and nesting. Integrating any of these preprocessors into your workflow will help you write cleaner and more maintainable stylesheets.

Section 10.4: PostCSS and Optimizing CSS

PostCSS is not a CSS preprocessor like Sass, LESS, or Stylus. Instead, it is often referred to as a "CSS post-processor" or "CSS transformer." PostCSS operates on already generated CSS, allowing you to apply various transformations and optimizations to your stylesheets. In this section, we will explore PostCSS and its capabilities for optimizing CSS.

What Is PostCSS?

PostCSS is a JavaScript-based tool that takes CSS as input, parses it into an abstract syntax tree (AST), processes it with various plugins, and then generates optimized CSS as output. It's highly modular and extensible, allowing you to choose from a wide range of plugins to tailor your optimization pipeline to your specific needs.

Benefits of PostCSS

Here are some benefits of using PostCSS for optimizing CSS:

1. **Modularity**: PostCSS is built around the concept of plugins, which means you can choose and configure only the optimizations you need. This modularity allows for a lightweight and customized approach to CSS

optimization.

2. **Browser Compatibility**: PostCSS plugins often include features like autoprefixing, which automatically adds vendor prefixes to CSS rules, ensuring cross-browser compatibility. This helps eliminate the need for manually writing and maintaining vendor-specific CSS.

3. **Performance**: PostCSS can perform various optimizations that can significantly reduce the size of your CSS files. This includes removing unused CSS, minification, and more.

4. **Future-Proofing**: PostCSS can transform your CSS to use the latest CSS specifications, even if they are not fully supported in all browsers. This ensures that your styles remain compatible with future web standards.

Common PostCSS Plugins

PostCSS has a vast ecosystem of plugins, each designed to address specific aspects of CSS optimization. Some common PostCSS plugins include:

- **Autoprefixer**: Adds vendor prefixes to CSS rules based on browser compatibility requirements.

- **cssnano**: A CSS minifier that removes whitespace, optimizes and compresses your stylesheets.

- **PostCSS Preset Env**: Allows you to use the latest CSS features by transforming them into browser-compatible CSS.

- **css-mqpacker**: Combines and optimizes CSS media queries to reduce redundancy.

- **PostCSS Custom Properties**: Provides support for CSS custom properties (variables) in older browsers.

- **PostCSS Flexbugs Fixes**: Addresses various flexbox-related bugs and inconsistencies in different browsers.

Setting Up PostCSS

To use PostCSS in your project, you typically follow these steps:

1. **Install PostCSS and Required Plugins**: Use npm or yarn to install PostCSS and the specific plugins you need for your project.
2. **Create a Configuration File**: Create a postcss.config.js or postcss.config.json file in your project's root directory. This file specifies the plugins and their configurations.
3. **Run PostCSS**: Use a task runner or build tool (e.g., Gulp, Webpack, or npm scripts) to run PostCSS on your CSS files. The configuration file specifies the input and output directories.

Conclusion

PostCSS is a powerful tool for optimizing and transforming CSS. It provides a flexible and modular approach to CSS optimization, making it suitable for a wide range of projects. Whether you need to ensure browser compatibility, improve performance, or future-proof your styles, PostCSS can be a valuable addition to your web development toolkit.

Section 10.5: Integrating Build Tools with CSS

In modern web development, integrating build tools with CSS has become essential to streamline the development workflow, improve code quality, and optimize assets for production. In this section, we'll explore how build tools like Gulp, Webpack, and npm scripts can be used to enhance your CSS development process.

Why Use Build Tools for CSS?

Build tools offer several advantages when working with CSS:

1. **Automation**: Build tools automate repetitive tasks, such as compiling preprocessor code (e.g., Sass or Less), optimizing images, and minifying CSS files. This automation saves time and reduces the chance of human error.

2. **Code Modularity**: Build tools allow you to organize your CSS code into smaller, manageable modules or components. This promotes code reusability and maintainability.

3. **Asset Optimization**: You can use build tools to optimize assets like images and fonts. This includes image compression, lazy loading, and generating responsive image sets.

4. **Transpilation**: If you're using future CSS features or custom syntax (e.g., CSS-in-JS), build tools can transpile your code into browser-compatible CSS.

5. **Live Reload and Development Server**: Many build tools come with development servers and live-reloading capabilities, allowing you to see instant updates as you make changes to your CSS.

Popular Build Tools for CSS

Here are some widely used build tools for CSS:

1. Gulp:

Gulp is a JavaScript task runner that excels at automating tasks like CSS compilation, minification, and image optimization. You can create custom Gulp tasks or use existing plugins to enhance your workflow.

Example Gulp task for CSS minification:

```
const gulp = require('gulp');

const cleanCSS = require('gulp-clean-css');

gulp.task('minify-css', () => {

return gulp.src('src/css/*.css')

.pipe(cleanCSS())

.pipe(gulp.dest('dist/css'));

});
```

2. Webpack:

Webpack is a powerful module bundler that can handle not only JavaScript but also CSS and other assets. It's commonly used in modern front-end development to bundle, optimize, and transpile CSS alongside JavaScript.

Webpack configuration for CSS (webpack.config.js):

```
module.exports = {

entry: './src/index.js',

output: {

filename: 'bundle.js',

path: path.resolve(__dirname, 'dist'),

},

module: {

rules: [

{

test: /\.css$/,

use: ['style-loader', 'css-loader'],

},

],

},

};
```

3. npm Scripts:

You can leverage npm scripts, defined in your project's package.json file, to run various CSS-related tasks using command-line tools. This approach is lightweight and easy to set up.

Example package.json scripts for CSS compilation using Sass:

```
{

"scripts": {

"build-css": "sass src/styles/main.scss dist/styles/main.css",

"watch-css": "sass src/styles/main.scss dist/styles/main.css—watch"

}

}
```

Integration with CSS Preprocessors and Postprocessors

Build tools can seamlessly integrate with CSS preprocessors like Sass, Less, and Stylus. You can configure your build process to compile preprocessor code into standard CSS automatically.

Moreover, you can integrate postprocessors like PostCSS into your build pipeline to optimize and transform the generated CSS.

Conclusion

Integrating build tools with CSS is crucial for modern web development. Whether you choose Gulp, Webpack, npm scripts, or other tools, automation and optimization will enhance your CSS development process, resulting in more efficient and maintainable code. By embracing these tools, you can stay up to date with the latest web development best practices and deliver high-quality CSS for your web projects.

Chapter 11: Cross-Browser Compatibility

Section 11.1: Dealing with Browser Differences

Cross-browser compatibility is a crucial aspect of web development. When you create a website or web application, you want it to work smoothly and consistently across various web browsers, including popular ones like Chrome, Firefox, Safari, Edge, and even older versions of Internet Explorer. However, different browsers may interpret CSS and HTML in slightly different ways, which can lead to rendering issues and inconsistencies. In this section, we'll explore strategies for dealing with these browser differences and ensuring your web projects look and function as intended.

Browser Detection vs. Feature Detection

One common approach to address browser differences is browser detection. This involves identifying the user's browser and version and applying specific fixes or workarounds based on that information. While this method can work, it's generally discouraged because it can lead to code that's difficult to maintain and prone to errors. Instead, a better approach is feature detection.

Feature detection involves checking if a specific browser supports a particular feature or property rather than identifying the browser itself. This approach is more reliable because it focuses on the capabilities of the browser rather than its name and version. JavaScript libraries like Modernizr can help with feature detection by providing a simple way to test for browser support.

// Example of feature detection using Modernizr

```
if (Modernizr.flexbox) {

// Browser supports flexbox

// Apply flexbox layout styles

} else {

// Fallback styles for browsers without flexbox support

}
```

CSS Resets and Normalization

CSS resets and normalization are techniques used to establish a consistent baseline for styling across different browsers. CSS resets aim to remove default browser styles to ensure a clean slate for your custom styles. On the other hand, CSS normalization aims to preserve some default styles but make them consistent across browsers.

Popular CSS reset libraries like Reset CSS and Normalize.css provide pre-built styles that you can include in your project to address common browser inconsistencies.

Vendor Prefixes and Autoprefixer

Vendor prefixes are used to apply experimental or non-standard CSS properties and features in different browsers. While these prefixes were necessary in the past, many CSS features have become standardized, and modern browsers no longer require them. However, for compatibility with older browsers, you may still encounter situations where vendor prefixes are needed.

Autoprefixer is a valuable tool that automatically adds the necessary vendor prefixes to your CSS based on the specified browser support.

By using Autoprefixer as part of your build process, you can ensure your CSS works seamlessly across a wide range of browsers without manually adding prefixes.

Polyfills for CSS3 Features

Polyfills are scripts or code snippets that provide support for modern CSS and JavaScript features in older browsers that lack native support. They enable you to use CSS3 features, such as transitions, animations, and flexbox, even in browsers that don't natively support these capabilities.

For instance, the "css3-transitions" polyfill can be used to add transition effects in browsers that don't support CSS3 transitions. When implementing polyfills, it's essential to include them selectively based on feature detection to avoid unnecessary overhead in browsers that don't need them.

In conclusion, cross-browser compatibility is essential for delivering a consistent and user-friendly web experience. By focusing on feature detection, using CSS resets and normalization, handling vendor prefixes, and leveraging polyfills when necessary, you can minimize the challenges posed by browser differences and ensure your web projects perform well across the browser landscape.

Section 11.2: CSS Resets and Normalization

When dealing with cross-browser compatibility in web development, one of the common challenges is browser-specific default styles. Each web browser applies its default styling to HTML elements, which can lead to inconsistencies in how your web pages are displayed. To address this issue and create a more uniform starting point for your CSS styles, you can use CSS resets and normalization techniques.

CSS Resets

A CSS reset is a set of CSS rules that aim to remove or reset browser-specific default styles on HTML elements. The goal is to create a level playing field by zeroing out default margins, paddings, fonts, and other styles applied by browsers. CSS resets help ensure that your CSS styles are applied consistently across different browsers.

Here's an example of a simple CSS reset:

```
/* CSS Reset */

* {

margin: 0;

padding: 0;

border: 0;

font-size: 100%;

font-family: inherit;

vertical-align: baseline;

}
```

In this reset, the * selector targets all elements on the page and resets properties like margins, padding, borders, font size, font family, and vertical alignment. While this approach provides a clean slate for styling, it can also be quite aggressive and may remove styles you want to keep.

Normalize.css

Normalize.css is an alternative to CSS resets. Instead of completely removing default styles, it aims to make default styles consistent across different browsers. Normalize.css preserves useful default styles, such as formatting for headings and lists, while ensuring consistency in rendering.

You can include Normalize.css in your project by linking to it in your HTML file's <head> section:

<link rel="stylesheet" href="normalize.css">

Here's an example of how Normalize.css normalizes default styles:

```
/* Normalize default styles */
html {
line-height: 1.15; /* 1 */
-webkit-text-size-adjust: 100%; /* 2 */
}
```

Normalize.css focuses on maintaining a balance between consistency and preserving useful default styles, making it a popular choice for many web developers.

Choosing Between Reset and Normalize

The choice between using a CSS reset and Normalize.css depends on your project's requirements and your design philosophy. If you prefer complete control over styles and want to start from scratch, a CSS reset may be more suitable. However, be prepared to redefine many default styles yourself.

On the other hand, if you want a more consistent and less intrusive approach that preserves some default styles, Normalize.css can be a better choice. It provides a solid foundation while allowing you to build upon it with your custom styles.

In conclusion, CSS resets and normalization techniques are valuable tools for achieving cross-browser compatibility by addressing default style inconsistencies. The choice between a reset and normalization should align with your project's goals and your preferences regarding how to handle default browser styles.

Section 11.3: Vendor Prefixes and Autoprefixer

When working with CSS for cross-browser compatibility, one of the challenges is dealing with vendor-specific CSS properties. Different web browsers often implement experimental or non-standard CSS properties with prefixes to indicate their origin. For example, you may encounter properties like -webkit-border-radius (used by WebKit-based browsers like Chrome and Safari) or -moz-border-radius (used by Mozilla Firefox).

The purpose of these prefixes is to allow browser vendors to experiment with new CSS features before they become standardized. However, this can lead to a situation where you need to write multiple versions of a CSS property to support different browsers. This can make your CSS code verbose and hard to maintain.

Vendor Prefixes

Vendor prefixes are specific to individual browser engines, and they are typically used for CSS properties that are not part of the official CSS standard or are still in experimental stages. While using vendor prefixes can ensure compatibility with specific browsers, it can also result in redundancy in your CSS code.

Here's an example of how you might apply vendor prefixes for the border-radius property:

/* Vendor prefixes for border-radius */

.example {

-webkit-border-radius: 10px; /* Chrome, Safari, Opera */

-moz-border-radius: 10px; /* Firefox */

border-radius: 10px; /* Standard */

}

As shown in the example, you need to specify the property with prefixes for different browsers in addition to the standard property without a prefix.

Autoprefixer

To simplify the process of adding and managing vendor prefixes in your CSS code, you can use a tool called Autoprefixer. Autoprefixer is a PostCSS plugin that automatically adds the necessary vendor prefixes based on your specified browser support.

Here's how you can use Autoprefixer:

1. **Installation**: You need to install Autoprefixer as a development dependency in your project. You can do this using npm or yarn:

   npm install autoprefixer—save-dev

 # or

yarn add autoprefixer—dev

1. **Configuration**: Create a configuration file, such as
   .browserslistrc in your project's root directory, to specify
   the browsers you want to support. For example:

> 1%

last 2 versions

not dead

This configuration means you want to support the last
two versions of popular browsers, as well as any browser
with more than 1% global usage.

1. **Usage**: You can use Autoprefixer in your CSS build
   process. For example, if you're using a task runner like
   Gulp, you can set up a PostCSS task that includes
   Autoprefixer. Here's a simplified example:

```
const gulp = require('gulp');

const postcss = require('gulp-postcss');

const autoprefixer = require('autoprefixer');

gulp.task('styles', () => {

const plugins = [

autoprefixer()
```

```
];

return gulp.src('src/css/*.css')

.pipe(postcss(plugins))

.pipe(gulp.dest('dist/css'));

});
```

When you run the styles task, Autoprefixer will automatically add the appropriate vendor prefixes based on your browser support configuration.

Benefits of Autoprefixer

Using Autoprefixer offers several benefits:

1. **Saves Time**: Autoprefixer automates the process of adding vendor prefixes, saving you time and effort.
2. **Reduces Errors**: It reduces the likelihood of errors or omissions when manually adding prefixes.
3. **Maintains Cleaner Code**: Your CSS code remains clean and concise without excessive vendor prefixes.
4. **Keeps Code Up-to-Date**: Autoprefixer can update vendor prefixes as browsers evolve, ensuring your styles remain compatible with new browser versions.

In conclusion, dealing with vendor prefixes can be cumbersome, but Autoprefixer simplifies the process and helps you maintain cleaner and more maintainable CSS code while ensuring cross-browser compatibility. Consider integrating Autoprefixer into your CSS build process to streamline your development workflow.

Section 11.4: Feature Detection and Modernizr

In the realm of web development, creating a consistent user experience across various browsers and devices can be challenging. Browsers differ in their support for HTML, CSS, and JavaScript features, and this can lead to compatibility issues. Feature detection is a crucial technique used to address these challenges, and one tool that aids in feature detection is Modernizr.

What Is Feature Detection?

Feature detection is a method employed by web developers to determine whether a specific browser or device supports a particular web technology or feature. Unlike browser detection, which tries to identify the user's browser and version, feature detection focuses on identifying whether a specific capability is available.

Here's a simple example of feature detection in JavaScript:

```
if (typeof window.localStorage !== 'undefined') {

// Local Storage is supported

// You can use localStorage to store data

} else {

// Local Storage is not supported

// Provide an alternative solution or inform the user

}
```

In this code snippet, we check if the localStorage object exists in the window object. If it does, it means the browser supports local storage.

Introducing Modernizr

Modernizr is a popular JavaScript library that simplifies feature detection. It works by adding classes to the HTML <html> element based on the features supported by the user's browser. Developers can then use these classes to apply CSS styles or execute JavaScript code conditionally.

How to Use Modernizr

1. **Installation**: You can include Modernizr in your project by downloading it from the Modernizr website[1] or by using package managers like npm or yarn.
2. **Initialization**: Include the Modernizr script in your HTML document before any other scripts. For example:

<script src="modernizr.js"**></**/**script>**

1. **Feature Detection**: Modernizr automatically adds classes to the <html> element based on the browser's capabilities. For example, if you want to check for CSS Flexbox support:

.flexbox .item {

/* Styles for browsers that support Flexbox */

}

---

1. https://modernizr.com/download

```
.no-flexbox .item {
```

/ Styles for browsers that do not support Flexbox */*

```
}
```

In this example, if the browser supports Flexbox, the flexbox class will be added to the <html> element, and the appropriate styles will be applied.

1. **JavaScript Testing**: Modernizr also provides a JavaScript API to programmatically check for features. For instance:

if (Modernizr.flexbox) {

// Flexbox is supported

// Execute code that relies on Flexbox

} **else** {

// Provide a fallback or alternative solution

}

You can use this approach to conditionally execute JavaScript code based on feature support.

Benefits of Using Modernizr

Modernizr offers several advantages:

1. **Granular Detection**: It allows you to perform feature detection at a granular level, checking for specific HTML, CSS, or JavaScript features.

2. **Cross-Browser Compatibility**: Modernizr helps ensure that your web application or site works consistently across various browsers.

3. **Progressive Enhancement**: Feature detection encourages the practice of progressive enhancement, where you build your web experiences with a baseline of functionality and enhance them for browsers that support advanced features.

4. **Conditional Loading**: You can conditionally load assets (such as CSS or JavaScript) based on feature detection, optimizing performance.

5. **Maintainability**: Modernizr simplifies the process of adapting your codebase to changing browser capabilities.

In summary, Modernizr is a valuable tool for web developers looking to build modern, feature-rich websites while maintaining compatibility with older browsers. By using feature detection techniques facilitated by Modernizr, you can create a more resilient and inclusive web experience for your users.

Section 11.5: Polyfills for CSS3 Features

Polyfills are JavaScript scripts or libraries that provide modern web features to older browsers that lack support for those features. While polyfills are commonly associated with JavaScript APIs, they can also be used to add support for CSS3 features in older browsers. In this section, we'll explore how polyfills can be employed to bridge the gap between older browsers and the latest CSS3 capabilities.

Why Use CSS3 Polyfills?

1. **Cross-Browser Compatibility**: One of the primary reasons for using CSS3 polyfills is to ensure cross-browser compatibility. Older browsers, especially Internet Explorer

(IE) versions 8 and below, lack support for many CSS3 features. Polyfills enable developers to provide consistent experiences to users regardless of their browser choice.

2. **Progressive Enhancement**: Polyfills align with the principle of progressive enhancement, where you start with a baseline experience for all users and then enhance it for modern browsers. This approach allows websites to remain functional in older browsers while providing richer experiences in newer ones.

3. **Future-Proofing**: By using CSS3 polyfills, you future-proof your websites. As more users transition to modern browsers, the need for polyfills decreases. Eventually, you can phase out polyfills when browser support for CSS3 features becomes widespread.

Popular CSS3 Polyfills

Let's look at a few popular CSS3 polyfills that address specific CSS3 features:

1. CSS3 PIE

CSS3 PIE (Progressive Internet Explorer) is a popular polyfill for Internet Explorer that adds support for several CSS3 features, including rounded corners, box shadows, and gradients. It works by rendering these CSS3 effects using JavaScript and VML (Vector Markup Language), making them compatible with older versions of IE.

Website: http://css3pie.com/

2. Selectivizr

Selectivizr is a JavaScript utility that provides support for CSS3 pseudo-classes like :nth-child, :last-child, and :first-child in IE 6-8. It extends the capabilities of these older browsers, allowing you to use advanced CSS3 selectors without compatibility issues.

GitHub Repository: https://github.com/keithclark/selectivizr

3. Respond.js

Respond.js is a lightweight polyfill that enables media query support in IE 6-8. It allows you to use responsive design techniques by making media queries functional in older browsers. This is especially useful for creating adaptive layouts.

GitHub Repository: https://github.com/scottjehl/Respond

4. CSS3-Multi-Column.js

CSS3-Multi-Column.js is a polyfill for CSS3 multi-column layouts. It extends support for multi-column text layouts to older browsers, enabling you to create magazine-style columns even in IE 6-9.

GitHub   Repository: https://github.com/danbentley/css3-multi-column.js

How to Use CSS3 Polyfills

Using CSS3 polyfills is relatively straightforward:

1. **Include the Polyfill Script**: Download the polyfill script and include it in your HTML document. Place it before your main CSS or JavaScript files. For example:

```
<script src="path/to/polyfill.js"></script>
```

1. **Apply CSS3 Features**: Write your CSS using the CSS3 features you want to polyfill. The polyfill will detect unsupported features in older browsers and make the necessary adjustments.
2. **Test Across Browsers**: Test your website in various browsers, including older versions of Internet Explorer, to ensure that the polyfill works as expected.
3. **Provide Fallbacks**: While polyfills can enhance older browsers, it's a good practice to provide graceful fallbacks for users who have JavaScript disabled or encounter issues with the polyfill.

Considerations

While CSS3 polyfills are a valuable tool for improving compatibility, they do come with some considerations:

- **Performance**: Polyfills introduce additional JavaScript code, which can impact page load times and responsiveness. Always evaluate the performance implications of using a polyfill.

- **Maintenance**: Keep track of updates and changes to the polyfills you use. As browser support improves, you may be able to remove or replace polyfills.

- **Feature Coverage**: Not all CSS3 features have polyfills available, so you may need to prioritize which features are most critical for your project.

In conclusion, CSS3 polyfills are a valuable resource for web developers striving to provide consistent and modern experiences across different browsers, especially when dealing with older versions of Internet Explorer. By carefully selecting and implementing polyfills, you can ensure that your web applications and sites remain accessible to a wide audience.

Chapter 12: CSS Frameworks and Libraries

Section 12.1: Introduction to CSS Frameworks

In the world of web development, CSS frameworks have become essential tools for building responsive and visually appealing websites efficiently. CSS frameworks are pre-prepared libraries of CSS code and sometimes JavaScript that provide a foundation for styling and structuring web pages. They offer a set of predefined styles, layout components, and responsive design patterns that developers can leverage to streamline the development process. In this section, we will introduce you to CSS frameworks, their benefits, and some popular examples.

What Are CSS Frameworks?

CSS frameworks are collections of reusable CSS styles and components that help developers maintain a consistent and visually appealing design throughout a website or web application. They provide a structured approach to web development by offering pre-designed elements like grids, buttons, typography, and form styles, saving developers from reinventing the wheel for common UI elements.

Benefits of Using CSS Frameworks

1. **Rapid Development**: CSS frameworks significantly speed up the development process by offering a ready-made set of styles and components. This means less time spent on writing custom CSS from scratch.

2. **Consistency**: Frameworks enforce a consistent design language across your project. This consistency is crucial for user experience and branding.

3. **Responsive Design**: Many CSS frameworks come with built-in responsive design features, making it easier to create websites that adapt to different screen sizes and devices.

4. **Community and Support**: Popular CSS frameworks have active communities and extensive documentation, making it easier to find help and resources when needed.

5. **Cross-Browser Compatibility**: Frameworks are often rigorously tested across various browsers, ensuring your website works consistently for your users.

Popular CSS Frameworks

Here are some well-known CSS frameworks that have gained popularity among web developers:

1. Bootstrap

Bootstrap is one of the most widely used CSS frameworks. It offers a comprehensive set of styles, components, and JavaScript plugins for building responsive web projects. Bootstrap's grid system, in particular, simplifies layout design.

Website: https://getbootstrap.com/

2. Foundation

Foundation is another popular CSS framework that focuses on creating responsive, mobile-first designs. It provides a flexible grid system, UI components, and JavaScript plugins.

Website: https://foundation.zurb.com/

3. Bulma

Bulma is a modern CSS framework that emphasizes simplicity and flexibility. It's built on a flexbox-based grid system and offers a clean and minimalistic design.

Website: https://bulma.io/

4. Semantic UI

Semantic UI aims to provide a framework that uses human-friendly HTML to create responsive and themable user interfaces. It encourages writing clean and semantic HTML while offering a wide range of UI components.

Website: https://semantic-ui.com/

5. Tailwind CSS

Tailwind CSS takes a different approach by providing a utility-first CSS framework. It offers a vast set of utility classes that you can apply directly to HTML elements, giving you complete control over your styles.

Website: https://tailwindcss.com/

Choosing the Right CSS Framework

When selecting a CSS framework for your project, consider factors like the project's requirements, design preferences, and your team's familiarity with the framework. Each CSS framework has its own strengths and weaknesses, so choose the one that aligns with your specific needs and workflow.

In the next sections of this chapter, we will delve deeper into specific CSS frameworks and how to use them effectively in your web development projects.

Section 12.2: Bootstrap: A Popular CSS Framework

Bootstrap is one of the most widely adopted CSS frameworks in the web development community. It was initially developed by Twitter and has since evolved into an open-source project with a vast community of contributors. Bootstrap is known for its robust set of CSS styles, responsive grid system, and a plethora of pre-designed components. In this section, we'll explore Bootstrap in more detail, including its key features and how to get started with it.

Key Features of Bootstrap

1. Responsive Grid System:

Bootstrap's grid system is based on a 12-column layout, which makes it easy to create responsive designs. You can define how many columns a specific element should span on different screen sizes, ensuring that your website looks great on various devices.

2. Pre-Designed Components:

Bootstrap provides a wide range of UI components, such as navigation bars, forms, buttons, alerts, and modals. These components come with default styles and behavior, saving you time and effort in styling and scripting.

3. Typography and Icons:

Bootstrap includes a typographic scale and a set of icons (Font Awesome) that you can easily incorporate into your designs. This ensures consistent typography and icon usage across your website.

4. Extensive Documentation:

Bootstrap has comprehensive documentation that covers its components, utilities, and CSS classes. You can quickly find information on how to use specific features and elements.

5. Customization:

While Bootstrap offers a predefined look and feel, it's highly customizable. You can customize the framework to match your project's branding by modifying variables and using its theming features.

Getting Started with Bootstrap

To start using Bootstrap in your project, follow these steps:

1. Include Bootstrap CSS and JavaScript:

Add Bootstrap's CSS and JavaScript files to your HTML document. You can either download Bootstrap and host the files locally or include them from a Content Delivery Network (CDN).

```
<!—Include Bootstrap CSS—>
```

```
<link href="https://cdn.jsdelivr.net/npm/bootstrap@5.5.0/dist/css/bootstrap.min.css" rel="stylesheet">
```

<!—Include Bootstrap JavaScript (optional)—>

<script   src="https://cdn.jsdelivr.net/npm/bootstrap@5.5.0/dist/js/bootstrap.min.js"**></script>**

2. *Start Building with Bootstrap:*

Once you've included the Bootstrap files, you can start using Bootstrap components and classes in your HTML. For example, to create a basic Bootstrap navbar, you can use the following code:

<nav class="navbar navbar-expand-lg navbar-light bg-light"**>**

<a class="navbar-brand" **href**="#"**>**My Website**</a>**

<button   class="navbar-toggler"   **type**="button"
data-toggle="collapse"   **data-target**="#navbarNav"
aria-controls="navbarNav"   **aria-expanded**="false"
aria-label="Toggle navigation"**>**

<span class="navbar-toggler-icon"**></span>**

</button>

<div class="collapse navbar-collapse" **id**="navbarNav"**>**

<ul class="navbar-nav"**>**

<li class="nav-item active"**>**

<a   class="nav-link"   **href**="#"**>**Home   **<span
class**="sr-only"**>**(current)**</span></a>**

</li>

<li class="nav-item"**>**

```html
<a class="nav-link" href="#">About</a>

</li>

<li class="nav-item">

<a class="nav-link" href="#">Services</a>

</li>

<li class="nav-item">

<a class="nav-link" href="#">Contact</a>

</li>

</ul>

</div>

</nav>
```

3. Customize Bootstrap (Optional):

If you want to customize Bootstrap's appearance, you can use the official Bootstrap customization tool, which allows you to adjust variables such as colors, fonts, and spacing. After customization, you can download a customized version of Bootstrap.

Conclusion

Bootstrap is an excellent choice for developers looking to quickly prototype or build responsive websites. Its comprehensive documentation and active community make it easy to learn and integrate into your projects. By understanding the key features and how to get started with Bootstrap, you can leverage its power to create stylish and responsive web applications efficiently.

Section 12.3: Foundation and Bulma: Alternatives to Bootstrap

While Bootstrap is a popular CSS framework, there are alternatives available that offer different features and approaches to front-end development. Two notable alternatives are **Foundation** and **Bulma**. In this section, we'll explore these frameworks and what sets them apart from Bootstrap.

Foundation CSS Framework

Foundation is a responsive front-end framework developed by ZURB. It's known for its flexibility and the ability to create highly customized designs. Here are some key features of Foundation:

1. **Mobile-First**: Foundation follows a mobile-first approach, ensuring that your designs look great on small screens and progressively enhance to larger devices.
2. **Responsive Grid System**: Similar to Bootstrap, Foundation offers a responsive grid system that simplifies layout creation.
3. **Modular Components**: Foundation provides a set of modular components, such as navigation menus, forms, and buttons. You can selectively include only the components you need, reducing unnecessary bloat.
4. **Customizable**: Foundation is highly customizable through Sass variables and mixins. You can easily change colors, fonts, and other design elements to match your project's branding.
5. **Theming**: Foundation includes a theming system that allows you to create themes and apply them to your projects. This makes it easy to maintain a consistent design across multiple websites.

Getting Started with Foundation

To start using Foundation, you need to include its CSS and JavaScript files in your HTML document. You can choose to download Foundation or use a CDN to include the files. Foundation also offers a command-line tool called Foundation CLI to streamline project setup.

Bulma CSS Framework

Bulma is a modern CSS framework based on Flexbox. It's known for its simplicity and lightweight nature. Here are some key features of Bulma:

1. **Flexbox-Based**: Bulma's layout system is entirely based on Flexbox, making it easy to create complex layouts and align elements.
2. **Minimalistic**: Bulma takes a minimalistic approach and provides a clean and simple set of styles. This makes it a great choice for projects where you want to avoid the extra styling that comes with larger frameworks.
3. **Modular**: Bulma is modular, allowing you to include only the parts of the framework that you need. This keeps your project lightweight and ensures that you're not loading unnecessary styles.
4. **Responsive**: Like other frameworks, Bulma is designed to be responsive out of the box, ensuring your designs adapt well to different screen sizes.

Getting Started with Bulma

To use Bulma in your project, you can include its CSS file in your HTML document. You can either download Bulma or include it via a CDN. Bulma also offers a command-line tool called Bulma CLI for project setup and customization.

Choosing Between Frameworks

When deciding between Bootstrap, Foundation, Bulma, or other CSS frameworks, consider your project requirements and design preferences. Bootstrap is an excellent choice for projects that need a robust set of pre-designed components and a large community. Foundation offers flexibility and customization options, while Bulma is ideal for minimalistic, lightweight designs. Ultimately, the choice depends on your specific project needs and your familiarity with the framework.

Section 12.4: Customizing CSS Frameworks

Customization is a crucial aspect of working with CSS frameworks. While frameworks like Bootstrap, Foundation, and Bulma offer predefined styles and components, you often need to customize them to match your project's unique design requirements. In this section, we'll explore how to customize CSS frameworks effectively.

Why Customize a CSS Framework?

There are several reasons why you might want to customize a CSS framework:

1. **Branding**: To ensure your website aligns with your brand's visual identity, you'll need to customize the framework's default styles, such as colors, typography, and logos.
2. **Unique Design**: Frameworks provide a starting point, but your project may require a unique design that can't be achieved with default styles alone.
3. **Performance**: Removing unnecessary styles and

components from a framework can improve your website's performance by reducing file sizes and HTTP requests.

4. **Responsiveness**: Customization allows you to fine-tune the framework's responsive behavior to ensure it adapts perfectly to different screen sizes and devices.

Customization Techniques

Here are some common techniques for customizing CSS frameworks:

1. Sass Variables

Many CSS frameworks, including Bootstrap and Foundation, use Sass or SCSS as their preprocessor. You can leverage this by modifying Sass variables to control aspects like colors, fonts, and spacing. Here's an example of changing the primary color in Bootstrap:

$primary-color: #007bff; // New primary color

@**import** 'bootstrap'; // Import Bootstrap styles

2. Custom Stylesheets

Create a custom stylesheet to override framework styles. Place your custom CSS rules after including the framework's CSS. This way, your styles will take precedence. For example:

<**link**   **rel**="stylesheet"   **href**="bootstrap.css">   <!—Include Bootstrap—>

<**link**   **rel**="stylesheet"   **href**="custom.css">   <!—Include custom styles—>

3. Component Overrides

Frameworks often provide guidelines for customizing specific components. Check the documentation for details on how to override individual components. For example, Bootstrap's documentation explains how to customize its navbar.

4. Utility Classes

Many frameworks offer utility classes that allow you to apply specific styles directly in your HTML markup. This can be handy for making quick adjustments without writing custom CSS. However, use them judiciously to avoid cluttering your HTML with presentation concerns.

Best Practices for Customization

When customizing a CSS framework, follow these best practices:

1. **Keep an Organized Workflow**: Maintain a structured approach to customization. Create a separate custom stylesheet or Sass file to avoid modifying framework files directly.
2. **Document Your Changes**: Clearly document your customizations. This helps you and your team understand the changes made and simplifies future updates.
3. **Version Control**: Use version control (e.g., Git) to track changes to your custom styles. This ensures you can roll back or review modifications easily.
4. **Test Thoroughly**: After making customizations, thoroughly test your website on different devices and browsers to ensure everything remains functional and visually appealing.

5. **Stay Informed**: Keep an eye on updates and releases from the framework's maintainers. Updates may introduce new features or security patches that you'll want to incorporate into your customized version.

Remember that while customization allows you to tailor a CSS framework to your project's needs, it also adds maintenance overhead. Striking the right balance between customization and ease of maintenance is essential for a successful project.

Section 12.5: Using CSS Libraries for Special Effects

In addition to CSS frameworks, you can leverage CSS libraries to add special effects and enhanced interactivity to your web projects. CSS libraries are collections of pre-built CSS styles and animations that can save you time and effort when implementing advanced design features. In this section, we'll explore some popular CSS libraries and how to use them effectively.

Popular CSS Libraries

1. Animate.css

Animate.css[1] is a well-known CSS animation library that provides a wide range of predefined animations. It's easy to use; you simply include the library in your project and apply CSS classes to elements you want to animate. For example, to add a bounce animation to a button, you can do the following:

<link **rel**="stylesheet" **href**="animate.css"> *<!—Include Animate.css—>*

---

1. https://animate.style/

```html
<button class="animate__animated animate__bounce">Animated
Button</button>
```

2. Hover.css

Hover.css[2] is another library for creating stylish hover effects. It offers a variety of transition effects that can be applied to buttons, links, and other elements. Here's an example of using Hover.css to add a "pulse" effect to a button:

```html
<link rel="stylesheet" href="hover.css"> <!—Include Hover.css—>

<button class="hvr-pulse">Hover Me</button>
```

3. Magic Animations

Magic Animations[3] is a library that provides a set of CSS animations designed for user interfaces. It offers smooth and subtle animations to enhance the user experience. To use Magic Animations, include the library and apply its classes as needed:

```html
<link rel="stylesheet" href="magic.css"> <!—Include Magic
Animations—>

<div class="magic">

<p class="magictime puffIn">Animated Text</p>

</div>
```

Applying CSS Libraries

To apply CSS libraries to your project, follow these general steps:

---

2. http://ianlunn.github.io/Hover/

3. https://www.minimamente.com/project/magic/

1. **Download or Include the Library**: Start by downloading the CSS file for the library you want to use or include it from a content delivery network (CDN) if available. Make sure to place the <link> tag in the <head> section of your HTML file.

2. **Add Required HTML Elements**: Include the HTML elements or components that you want to animate or apply special effects to. Add the necessary CSS classes or attributes to these elements to trigger the effects.

3. **Test and Customize**: Test the effects in your project, and customize them as needed. CSS libraries often provide documentation with customization options, allowing you to adjust the animation speed, duration, and other parameters to fit your design.

4. **Responsive Considerations**: Ensure that the effects are responsive and work well on various screen sizes and devices. You may need to make adjustments to the library's default settings to achieve this.

5. **Performance**: While CSS libraries can add visually appealing effects, be mindful of their impact on performance. Minimize unnecessary animations, and consider using JavaScript to control animations only when they are visible in the viewport.

6. **Accessibility**: Ensure that the animations do not hinder accessibility. For example, if you use animations for buttons or links, make sure they are still usable and understandable by screen readers and keyboard users.

Conclusion

CSS libraries can be valuable tools for adding special effects and animations to your web projects. They save you time and effort by providing pre-built styles and animations that enhance user engagement and interactivity. However, it's essential to use these libraries judiciously, keeping performance, accessibility, and responsiveness in mind to create a positive user experience.

Chapter 13: Accessibility and Inclusive Design

Section 13.1: Understanding Web Accessibility

Web accessibility, often abbreviated as A11Y (pronounced as "ally"), refers to the practice of making web content and applications usable by people with disabilities. This essential aspect of web development ensures that individuals with varying disabilities can perceive, understand, navigate, and interact with web content effectively. Accessibility is not just a legal requirement in many regions but also a moral imperative and best practice for web developers.

Why Web Accessibility Matters

1. **Inclusivity**: The primary goal of web accessibility is to include everyone, regardless of their abilities. By creating accessible websites, you ensure that people with disabilities can access and use your content and services.

2. **Legal Compliance**: Many countries and regions have implemented accessibility standards and regulations, such as the Web Content Accessibility Guidelines (WCAG). Failure to comply with these standards can lead to legal consequences and penalties.

3. **Business Benefits**: Accessible websites can reach a broader audience, potentially increasing your user base and customer base. Additionally, accessible design can improve search engine optimization (SEO) and user experience for all users.

4. **Ethical Responsibility**: Ensuring accessibility is a matter of ethical responsibility. It reflects your commitment to

treating all users fairly and equitably, promoting diversity and inclusion on the web.

Types of Disabilities

Web accessibility addresses a wide range of disabilities, including but not limited to:

• **Visual Disabilities**: This includes blindness, low vision, and color blindness. Screen readers and magnification tools help users with visual impairments navigate websites.

• **Hearing Disabilities**: Deafness and hearing impairments are considered in web accessibility. Providing captioning and transcripts for multimedia content is crucial.

• **Motor Disabilities**: People with motor impairments may use alternative input devices, such as switches or voice commands, to navigate websites. Ensuring keyboard accessibility is essential.

• **Cognitive Disabilities**: Individuals with cognitive impairments may have difficulty with complex navigation or comprehension. Clear and simple language and layouts are beneficial.

Web Content Accessibility Guidelines (WCAG)

The Web Content Accessibility Guidelines (WCAG) are a globally recognized set of recommendations and standards for creating accessible web content. These guidelines are organized into four key principles:

1. **Perceivable**: Information and user interface components must be presented in a way that users can perceive. This includes providing text alternatives for non-text content and ensuring content can be presented in various ways.
2. **Operable**: Users must be able to interact with the interface effectively. This involves keyboard navigation, providing ample time for tasks, and avoiding content that may cause seizures or physical discomfort.
3. **Understandable**: Information and the operation of user interface must be clear and understandable. This includes using consistent navigation and providing instructions when necessary.
4. **Robust**: Content must be robust enough to work with current and future technologies. This means using valid HTML, CSS, and JavaScript practices to ensure compatibility with assistive technologies.

Accessibility Testing and Tools

To ensure web accessibility, developers can use various tools and perform testing. Automated tools like accessibility checkers can identify common issues, but manual testing and user testing with people with disabilities are also essential for a comprehensive evaluation.

Conclusion

Web accessibility is not an option but a necessity in today's digital landscape. It's a commitment to creating a web that is open and inclusive to all users, regardless of their abilities. Understanding the principles of web accessibility, complying with guidelines like WCAG, and regularly testing your website's accessibility are vital steps in promoting an inclusive web. In the following sections, we will delve deeper into the techniques and best practices for achieving web accessibility and inclusive design.

Section 13.2: Semantic HTML and ARIA Roles

In the pursuit of web accessibility, the use of semantic HTML and ARIA (Accessible Rich Internet Applications) roles plays a pivotal role. Semantic HTML provides structure to web content, making it understandable for both humans and assistive technologies like screen readers. ARIA roles, on the other hand, allow developers to enhance the semantics of non-semantic elements, making them accessible.

Semantic HTML

Semantic HTML elements convey meaning about the structure of a web page. They help assistive technologies understand the content's hierarchy, purpose, and relationships. Here are some commonly used semantic elements:

- <header>: Represents introductory content or a set of navigational links.

- <nav>: Denotes a navigation menu.

- <main>: Signifies the main content area.

- <section>: Defines a thematic grouping of content.

- <article>: Represents a self-contained composition, such as a blog post or news article.

- <aside>: Represents content tangentially related to the surrounding content.

- <footer>: Represents the footer section of a page or a section.

By using these elements appropriately, you enhance the clarity and accessibility of your web pages. For instance, screen readers can identify the <nav> element as a navigation menu and allow users to skip directly to it, improving navigation efficiency.

ARIA Roles

While semantic HTML covers a significant portion of accessibility needs, there are situations where non-semantic elements are necessary for layout or interaction purposes. ARIA roles come into play here. ARIA roles and attributes are applied to HTML elements to define their roles, properties, and states in a way that assistive technologies can understand.

Some common ARIA roles include:

- role="button": Indicates an element as a clickable button.

- role="checkbox": Identifies an element as a checkbox.

- role="menu": Defines a container as a menu.

- role="tablist": Specifies a list of tabs.

- role="alert": Notifies users of important information or changes.

Here's an example of how ARIA can be used to enhance the accessibility of a button:

<button aria-label="Close" **onclick**="closeDialog()">X</**button**>

In this example, aria-label provides a textual label for the button since the content "X" alone may not convey its purpose to screen reader users.

Best Practices

To maximize the benefits of semantic HTML and ARIA roles:

1. **Prioritize Semantic Elements**: Whenever possible, use semantic HTML elements like <nav>, <main>, and <section> to structure your content.
2. **Provide Meaningful Labels**: Use alt attributes for images and aria-label for elements like buttons to provide descriptive labels.
3. **Use ARIA as a Last Resort**: Rely on ARIA roles only when semantic HTML elements are insufficient or inappropriate.
4. **Test with Assistive Technologies**: Regularly test your website with screen readers and other assistive technologies to ensure proper interpretation.

Incorporating semantic HTML and ARIA roles into your web development practices is a fundamental step toward creating a more accessible web. These techniques improve both the user experience and the ability of assistive technologies to convey the content's meaning to users with disabilities.

Section 13.3: Designing for Keyboard Navigation

Keyboard navigation is a critical aspect of web accessibility, ensuring that individuals who rely on keyboard input can fully and efficiently interact with your web content. Designing for keyboard navigation goes hand in hand with creating an inclusive web experience. Here are key considerations and best practices to make your web applications and sites keyboard-friendly.

1. Keyboard Focus Styles

Ensure that all interactive elements, such as links, buttons, and form fields, have a visible and consistent focus style. This is crucial for users navigating your site with a keyboard or other input devices. CSS styles like :focus should be used to highlight the focused element.

/ Example focus style for buttons */*

button:*focus* {

outline: 2px solid #007bff; */* Add a blue outline when focused */*

}

2. Skip Links

Include skip links at the beginning of your web pages to allow keyboard users to jump directly to main content, navigation menus, or other important sections. This is especially helpful for users who may need to navigate through repetitive elements.

<**a**   **href**="#main-content"   **class**="skip-link">Skip   to   Main Content</**a**>

/ Style for the skip link */*

.skip-link {

position: absolute;

left: -999em;

```
}
.skip-link:focus {
left: 0;
background-color: #007bff;
color: #fff;
padding: 5px;
z-index: 9999;
}
```

3. Logical Tab Order

Ensure that the tab order (the order in which elements receive focus when the user presses the "Tab" key) follows a logical sequence. Elements should be navigated in the order they appear on the page to provide a predictable experience.

4. Interactive Elements

All interactive elements, including dropdown menus, modal dialogs, and accordions, should be operable and accessible via the keyboard. Use appropriate ARIA roles and JavaScript event listeners to enhance keyboard support for these components.

5. Keyboard Traps

Avoid creating keyboard traps where users get stuck in a particular interface element. For example, if a modal dialog opens, make sure the user can navigate out of it using the keyboard.

// Example of allowing Esc key to close a modal

```
modalElement.addEventListener('keydown', function (event) {

if (event.key === 'Escape') {

closeModal();

}

});
```

6. Testing with Keyboard Navigation

Regularly test your website's keyboard navigation using only the keyboard, without relying on a mouse. Ensure that all functionality is accessible, and that users can perform essential actions, such as submitting forms and navigating menus.

7. Documentation

Include keyboard navigation instructions in your documentation or help sections, so users with disabilities can learn how to effectively interact with your site.

Designing for keyboard navigation is not only an accessibility requirement but also a good practice for creating web applications that work seamlessly for all users. By following these guidelines and considering the needs of keyboard users, you contribute to a more inclusive and user-friendly web experience.

Section 13.4: Testing for Accessibility Compliance

Ensuring that your website or web application meets accessibility standards is essential for providing an inclusive online experience for all users, including those with disabilities. Testing for accessibility compliance should be an integral part of your web development process. In this section, we'll explore various aspects of accessibility testing and the tools available to assist you in this endeavor.

1. Automated Accessibility Testing

Automated accessibility testing tools are designed to scan your web content and identify common accessibility issues. These tools can check for things like missing alt text for images, proper heading structure, and contrast ratios. Some popular automated accessibility testing tools include:

- axe[1] by Deque Systems: A widely-used open-source accessibility testing engine.

- WAVE[2]: A web-based tool that provides detailed reports on accessibility issues.

- Lighthouse[3]: Integrated into Google Chrome's DevTools, Lighthouse includes an accessibility audit.

These tools are valuable for quickly identifying and fixing common accessibility problems in your web content.

2. Manual Accessibility Testing

While automated tools are helpful, they can't catch all accessibility issues. Manual testing by individuals with expertise in accessibility is essential. Some aspects of manual testing include:

---

1. https://www.deque.com/axe/

2. https://wave.webaim.org/

3. https://developers.google.com/web/tools/lighthouse

- **Keyboard Testing**: Ensure that all interactive elements, such as buttons and forms, are fully operable using a keyboard only.

- **Screen Reader Testing**: Test your content with screen reader software like JAWS, NVDA, or VoiceOver to ensure that it's properly read aloud and navigable.

- **Semantic HTML**: Review your HTML code to ensure proper use of semantic elements like headings, lists, and landmarks.

- **Color Contrast**: Manually check text and background color contrast to ensure readability, especially for users with visual impairments.

3. Accessibility Guidelines

Familiarize yourself with accessibility guidelines and standards, such as the Web Content Accessibility Guidelines (WCAG) published by the W3C. WCAG provides a comprehensive set of recommendations for creating accessible web content. Aim for at least WCAG 2.1 AA compliance, which is a widely recognized standard.

4. User Testing

Involve individuals with disabilities in user testing to get direct feedback on your website's accessibility. They can provide insights into the user experience and uncover issues that automated tools may miss.

5. Accessibility Audit and Remediation

Regularly conduct accessibility audits of your website, addressing issues found during testing. Consider using issue tracking systems to manage and prioritize accessibility improvements.

6. Accessible Documentation

Provide accessible documentation and resources that educate your team about accessibility best practices. This helps ensure that everyone involved in the development process understands their role in creating an accessible product.

7. Accessibility in Development Workflow

Integrate accessibility checks into your development workflow. Tools like eslint-plugin-jsx-a11y for React or the Accessibility Insights extension for Visual Studio Code can help catch accessibility issues during development.

8. Continuous Learning

Accessibility is an evolving field. Stay up-to-date with the latest guidelines and best practices. Attend webinars, conferences, and workshops focused on accessibility to enhance your knowledge and skills.

Remember that accessibility is an ongoing commitment. Regular testing, user feedback, and a proactive approach to addressing accessibility concerns are crucial for creating a web environment that is inclusive and welcoming to all users.

Section 13.5: Inclusive Design Principles

Inclusive design goes beyond accessibility compliance. It focuses on creating products and experiences that are not only usable by people with disabilities but also enjoyable and beneficial for everyone, regardless of their abilities or limitations. In this section, we'll explore inclusive design principles and strategies for making your web projects more inclusive.

1. Understand Diverse User Needs

To create inclusive designs, it's crucial to understand the diverse needs and preferences of your users. This includes considering various disabilities (e.g., visual, auditory, motor, cognitive), different technological constraints, and varying contexts of use (e.g., mobile devices, screen readers, noisy environments).

2. Involve Diverse Stakeholders

Inclusive design benefits from involving a wide range of stakeholders, including people with disabilities. Their input and feedback can provide valuable insights into usability and accessibility challenges. Regularly engage with users through testing, surveys, and user interviews.

3. Flexibility and Personalization

Provide users with options to customize their experience. Allow them to adjust font sizes, color schemes, or the layout to better suit their needs and preferences. Personalization can greatly enhance the user experience for individuals with diverse requirements.

4. Clear and Consistent Interfaces

Create clear and consistent user interfaces that follow recognized design patterns. Consistency in layout, navigation, and interaction helps users, especially those with cognitive disabilities, understand and predict how your website or application works.

5. Prioritize Content and Features

Identify the most critical content and features, and ensure they are easily accessible and usable. Use progressive enhancement to deliver core functionality to all users and then enhance it for more capable devices or browsers.

6. Alternative Content

Provide alternative content for non-text elements like images, videos, and audio. Use descriptive alt text, captions, and transcripts to make multimedia content accessible to users with disabilities.

7. Keyboard Accessibility

Ensure that all interactive elements can be operated using a keyboard alone. Keyboard accessibility benefits users with motor impairments who rely on keyboard navigation.

8. Efficient Navigation

Implement clear and efficient navigation pathways. Use meaningful link text, organize content with headings, and provide skip navigation links to help users quickly find what they're looking for.

9. Test Across Devices and Browsers

Test your designs across a variety of devices, browsers, and assistive technologies to ensure compatibility. Different combinations can have varying levels of support for web standards and accessibility features.

10. Performance Optimization

Optimize your website or application for performance. Faster load times and smooth interactions benefit all users, especially those with limited bandwidth or older devices.

11. User Education and Support

Offer resources and support to educate users about accessibility features and how to use them. This can include tooltips, guides, or help sections that explain accessibility options.

12. Continuous Improvement

Inclusive design is an ongoing process. Regularly review and improve your designs based on user feedback, emerging technologies, and changes in best practices.

13. Promote Awareness

Raise awareness within your organization and among your team members about the importance of inclusive design. Encourage a culture of inclusivity and empathy in all aspects of product development.

Inclusive design isn't just a checkbox; it's a mindset and a commitment to creating digital experiences that welcome everyone. By incorporating these principles into your design and development process, you can help ensure that your web projects are accessible and beneficial to a broad and diverse audience.

Chapter 14: Performance Optimization for CSS

Section 14.1: Reducing CSS File Sizes

Efficient CSS plays a crucial role in optimizing the performance of your web pages. Smaller CSS files load faster, resulting in quicker page rendering and improved user experiences. In this section, we will explore strategies for reducing the file size of your CSS while maintaining its functionality.

1. Minification

Minification is the process of removing unnecessary characters (such as whitespace, comments, and line breaks) from your CSS files. Minification tools like CSS Minifier[1] or task runners like Grunt[2] and Gulp[3] can automate this process.

Before Minification:

body {

font-family: "Arial", sans-serif;

margin: 0;

padding: 0;

}

.header {

---

1. https://cssminifier.com/

2. https://gruntjs.com/

3. https://gulpjs.com/

background-color: #3498db;

color: white;

}

After Minification:

body{**font-family**:"Arial",sans-serif;**margin**:0;**padding**:0;}.header{**backgro**

2. CSS Compression

CSS compression involves using algorithms to further reduce the size of your CSS files. Popular CSS compression tools include CSSNano[4] and CleanCSS[5]. These tools can also perform minification as part of the process.

3. Remove Unused Code

Regularly review your CSS files and remove any rules or styles that are no longer in use. Unused code adds unnecessary weight to your stylesheets.

4. Combine CSS Files

If your website loads multiple CSS files, consider combining them into a single file. Fewer HTTP requests can lead to faster load times. Tools like Sass[6] and Less[7] make it easy to split your styles into manageable modules and then compile them into a single file for production.

---

4. https://cssnano.co/

5. https://github.com/jakubpawlowicz/clean-css

6. https://sass-lang.com/

7. http://lesscss.org/

5. Optimize Images in CSS

If your CSS references images, make sure they are optimized for the web. Tools like ImageOptim[8] can help reduce image file sizes without compromising quality.

6. Use CSS Sprites

CSS sprites involve combining multiple small images into a single image and then using CSS to display only the portion you need for each element. This reduces the number of image requests and can significantly improve loading times.

7. Avoid @import

Using the @import rule to load additional stylesheets can result in slower page loading because each imported file is loaded sequentially. Instead, use multiple <link> elements in your HTML to load CSS files in parallel.

8. Media Queries and Conditional Loading

Consider using media queries to load CSS files conditionally based on the user's device or screen size. This way, you can deliver optimized styles for specific situations without overloading the initial load.

9. Caching

Leverage browser caching by setting appropriate cache-control headers for your CSS files. This allows returning visitors to load the CSS from their cache rather than downloading it again.

---

8. https://imageoptim.com/

10. Content Delivery Networks (CDNs)

Use a CDN to distribute your CSS files. CDNs often have multiple servers worldwide, reducing latency and improving download speeds for users in different geographic locations.

Optimizing your CSS for performance is an essential aspect of web development. By following these strategies, you can ensure that your stylesheets are efficient, resulting in faster loading times and a better overall user experience for your website or web application.

Section 14.2: Minification and Compression

In Section 14.1, we discussed the importance of reducing CSS file sizes for better web performance. Now, let's dive deeper into the concepts of minification and compression, which are essential techniques for achieving smaller and more efficient CSS files.

1. Minification

Minification is the process of removing unnecessary characters and formatting from your CSS code without altering its functionality. The primary goal is to reduce file size and improve load times. Here are some key points about minification:

- **Whitespace Removal**: Minification eliminates spaces, tabs, and line breaks, making the CSS more compact. For example, a rule like margin: 10px 0; becomes margin:10px 0;.

- **Comments Removal**: Comments in CSS files, while helpful for developers, are not needed in production. Minification removes all comments, including /* ... */ and // ... comments.

- **Shortening Values**: Minification may also shorten values where possible. For instance, #FFFFFF might become #FFF if the shorter version represents the same color.

- **Semicolon Optimization**: Redundant semicolons are removed. For instance, font-weight: bold;; is corrected to font-weight: bold;.

Minification can be performed manually, but it's often automated using build tools or online services. Popular CSS minification tools include Terser[9], CSSNano[10], and UglifyCSS[11]. These tools ensure consistent and reliable minification.

2. Compression

While minification reduces file size by optimizing the structure of the CSS code, compression further reduces the size by using compression algorithms. Common compression techniques include Gzip and Brotli.

- **Gzip**: Gzip is widely supported by web servers and browsers. It compresses text-based files, including CSS, before they are transmitted over the network. When a browser requests a Gzipped CSS file, the server sends the compressed version, which is then decompressed by the browser. This results in faster downloads.

- **Brotli**: Brotli is a newer compression algorithm developed by Google. It is more efficient than Gzip and can achieve higher compression ratios. However, Brotli

---

9. https://terser.org/

10. https://cssnano.co/

11. https://github.com/GoalSmashers/cssmin

requires server-side support, and not all browsers support it for decompression.

To enable compression for your CSS files, you need to configure your web server to apply Gzip or Brotli compression. Most hosting providers offer this feature, and it's typically a matter of enabling it through server settings or a configuration file.

It's important to note that you can use both minification and compression together. Minify your CSS to remove unnecessary characters and then compress the minified file to further reduce its size. This combination ensures that your CSS files are as small as possible, leading to faster page loading times for your website or web application.

In summary, minification and compression are essential techniques for optimizing CSS files. Minification streamlines the code by removing unnecessary characters and formatting, while compression reduces the size even further through algorithms like Gzip and Brotli. By implementing these techniques, you can significantly improve the performance of your web projects.

Section 14.3: Critical CSS for Faster Page Loading

In Section 14.1, we explored the importance of reducing CSS file sizes through minification and compression. In this section, we'll delve into the concept of Critical CSS, a technique that plays a crucial role in improving web page loading performance.

1. Understanding Critical CSS

Critical CSS refers to the subset of CSS required to render the above-the-fold content of a web page. The "above-the-fold" content is the portion of the page that is visible to users without scrolling. Critical CSS is essential because it enables faster rendering of this initial view, resulting in a perceived performance boost.

When a web page loads, the browser parses HTML and encounters external CSS files linked in the <head> section. By default, browsers render the page only after they have downloaded and applied all the CSS. This can lead to a delay in rendering, especially if the CSS file is large or the user's network connection is slow.

Critical CSS addresses this issue by inlining or loading asynchronously the CSS required for the above-the-fold content. This allows the browser to begin rendering the visible portion of the page promptly. The remaining CSS can be loaded asynchronously or deferred for later rendering.

2. Generating Critical CSS

Generating Critical CSS can be done manually, but it's often automated using build tools or online services. Here are two common approaches:

- **Manual Extraction**: Manually identify the CSS rules required for the above-the-fold content and create a separate CSS file containing only these rules. This file is then inlined or loaded asynchronously.

- **Automated Tools**: Various tools and services can automate the process of generating Critical CSS. They analyze your web page and produce a CSS file tailored to the above-the-fold content. Popular tools include Critical CSS[12], Penthouse[13], and Webpack's critical-css plugin[14].

---

12. https://github.com/addyosmani/critical

13. https://github.com/pocketjoso/penthouse

3. Implementation Considerations

When implementing Critical CSS, consider the following:

- **Maintainability**: Keep the Critical CSS file up to date as your page's design evolves.

- **Cache Control**: Implement cache control headers to ensure the Critical CSS file is cached efficiently.

- **Fallback**: Provide a fallback mechanism for users with JavaScript disabled or for browsers that don't support asynchronous loading.

- **Testing**: Thoroughly test your implementation to ensure it doesn't negatively affect the layout or styling of your web page.

- **Responsive Design**: Adapt your Critical CSS for different screen sizes and devices.

- **Monitoring and Optimization**: Continuously monitor and optimize your Critical CSS to ensure it remains effective.

By implementing Critical CSS, you can significantly enhance the perceived performance of your web pages by reducing the time it takes for users to see and interact with your content. This technique is particularly valuable for improving the user experience on slower networks or less powerful devices.

---

14. https://github.com/anthonygore/html-critical-webpack-plugin

Section 14.4: Lazy Loading CSS Resources

In Section 14.3, we explored the concept of Critical CSS for faster page loading. In this section, we'll delve into another technique called lazy loading for CSS resources. Lazy loading is a strategy to improve page performance by deferring the loading of non-critical CSS until it's needed.

1. Understanding Lazy Loading CSS

Lazy loading CSS means postponing the retrieval and application of certain CSS files until they are required for the current user's interaction with the page. This approach reduces the initial loading time and allows the user to see and interact with the page faster.

The primary goal of lazy loading CSS is to prioritize the loading of critical resources, such as HTML, Critical CSS, and visible images, while deferring the loading of non-essential CSS files that may be needed for less common interactions or specific sections of a web page.

2. Benefits of Lazy Loading CSS

Lazy loading CSS offers several advantages:

- **Faster Initial Load**: By loading only critical CSS initially, the page becomes visible and interactive more quickly.

- **Reduced Data Usage**: Users on limited data plans benefit from reduced initial data consumption.

- **Improved Page Speed**: Faster loading times lead to better user experience and potentially higher search engine rankings.

3. Implementing Lazy Loading CSS

To implement lazy loading for CSS, you can follow these general steps:

a. Identify Non-Critical CSS

First, identify the CSS files or styles that are not essential for the initial rendering of your page. This typically includes styles for components like modals, off-canvas menus, or less frequently accessed content.

b. Load CSS Asynchronously

To load CSS files asynchronously, you can use JavaScript to create <link> elements with the appropriate rel and href attributes. Here's a simplified example:

```
<script>

const link = document.createElement('link');

link.rel = 'stylesheet';

link.href = 'non-critical.css';

document.head.appendChild(link);

</script>
```

c. Trigger Loading

You can trigger the loading of non-critical CSS files based on user interactions or when certain conditions are met. For example, you might load additional styles when a user clicks a button to open a modal.

d. *Testing and Optimization*

Test your lazy loading implementation thoroughly to ensure it doesn't interfere with the page's layout or functionality. Monitor performance and optimize as needed.

4. Considerations and Best Practices

When implementing lazy loading for CSS, keep the following considerations in mind:

- Balance: Strive to find the right balance between loading critical CSS immediately and deferring non-critical CSS.

- User Experience: Ensure that user interactions, such as opening a modal, don't feel sluggish due to the delayed CSS loading.

- Compatibility: Check for browser compatibility and consider providing a fallback for browsers that don't support lazy loading techniques.

- SEO: Be aware that search engine crawlers may not execute JavaScript, so ensure critical styles are still available in the initial HTML.

By effectively implementing lazy loading for non-critical CSS resources, you can enhance the perceived performance of your web pages, especially for users with slower connections or less powerful devices. This approach contributes to a smoother and faster user experience.

Section 14.5: Measuring and Improving Performance

In this section, we will explore various techniques and tools for measuring and improving the performance of your CSS. Performance optimization is crucial for delivering a fast and responsive user experience, which is a key factor in retaining users and achieving high search engine rankings.

1. Performance Metrics

Before diving into optimization techniques, let's understand the performance metrics that are commonly used to assess the speed and efficiency of a web page:

a. Page Load Time (PLT)

Page load time measures how long it takes for a web page to fully load and become interactive. This is often the most critical metric for user experience.

b. Time to First Byte (TTFB)

TTFB measures the time it takes for a user's browser to receive the first byte of data from the web server. A shorter TTFB indicates faster server response times.

c. Render Start Time

This metric tracks when the browser starts rendering the page. An early render start time is essential for perceived performance.

d. Time to Interactive (TTI)

TTI measures when a web page becomes fully interactive. It's an important metric for ensuring that users can interact with your site without delays.

e. Total Blocking Time (TBT)

TBT measures the total amount of time during which the main thread is blocked, preventing user interactions. Lower TBT indicates better responsiveness.

f. Largest Contentful Paint (LCP)

LCP measures when the largest content element becomes visible. A fast LCP contributes to a positive user experience.

2. Performance Optimization Techniques

Now, let's explore some CSS-specific performance optimization techniques:

a. Minification and Compression

Minify your CSS by removing unnecessary spaces, comments, and redundant code. Additionally, use gzip or Brotli compression to reduce the file size during transmission.

b. Critical CSS

Implement Critical CSS by extracting and inlining styles needed for above-the-fold content. This ensures that essential styles load quickly.

c. Lazy Loading

Employ lazy loading for non-critical CSS and JavaScript resources, as discussed in Section 14.4. This defers loading until user interactions or specific conditions trigger it.

d. Responsive Images

Optimize images for different screen sizes and resolutions, serving smaller images to mobile devices and larger ones to desktops. Use the srcset attribute to provide multiple image versions.

e. Font Loading Strategies

Optimize font loading by using the font-display property to control how fonts are displayed while loading. This helps prevent the invisible text problem caused by font loading delays.

f. Async and Defer Attributes

Use the async and defer attributes for <script> tags to control when JavaScript files are executed. This can prevent JavaScript from blocking rendering.

3. Performance Testing Tools

To measure and analyze your website's performance, consider using the following tools:

a. Lighthouse

Lighthouse is a built-in tool in Google Chrome's DevTools that provides comprehensive performance audits, including metrics and recommendations for improvements.

b. PageSpeed Insights

PageSpeed Insights, also by Google, analyzes your web page's performance on both desktop and mobile devices and offers suggestions for optimization.

c. WebPageTest

WebPageTest allows you to test your website's performance from various locations and devices. It provides detailed waterfall charts and performance metrics.

d. GTmetrix

GTmetrix offers insights into your website's performance, including PageSpeed and YSlow scores, along with recommendations for optimization.

4. Performance Monitoring and Continuous Improvement

Performance optimization is an ongoing process. Monitor your website's performance regularly and address any issues that arise. Keep an eye on new performance optimization techniques and tools to stay up to date with best practices.

By applying these performance optimization techniques and using the right tools, you can ensure that your CSS and web pages load quickly and provide an exceptional user experience.

Chapter 15: CSS Best Practices and Code Organization

Section 15.1: Writing Clean and Maintainable CSS

When working on CSS for web projects, it's crucial to follow best practices to ensure your code is clean, maintainable, and scalable. Well-organized CSS not only makes your codebase more manageable but also facilitates collaboration with other developers. In this section, we'll explore various strategies and techniques for writing clean and maintainable CSS.

1. Use a Consistent Naming Convention

Consistency in naming CSS classes and IDs is fundamental. Adopting a naming convention, such as BEM (Block, Element, Modifier) or SMACSS (Scalable and Modular Architecture for CSS), can greatly improve code readability. It helps developers understand the purpose of each CSS rule.

```
/* Example using BEM */

.header {}

.header__logo {}

.header__menu {}

.header__menu—active {}
```

2. Avoid Overly Specific Selectors

Overly specific selectors can lead to specificity wars and make it challenging to override styles when needed. Favor using class and ID selectors over element selectors to keep specificity in check.

/* Avoid */

article div p {}

/* Prefer */

.article-content .paragraph {}

3. Keep Selectors Short and Descriptive

Choose selectors that are concise yet descriptive. Aim for clarity in your code. Avoid selecting elements by overly long paths through the HTML structure.

/* Better */

.button {}

/* Avoid */

.container .content .main-content .button {}

4. Use Comments Wisely

Comments are invaluable for explaining the purpose of CSS rules. They can provide context for other developers or even your future self. Be descriptive but not verbose in your comments.

/* Good use of comments */

/* Header styles */

.header {}

/* Footer styles */

.footer {}

5. Group Related Properties

Grouping related properties together makes your CSS more readable. For instance, group all font-related properties together, followed by positioning properties, etc.

/* Group related properties */

.button {

font-family: Arial, sans-serif;

font-size: 16px;

font-weight: bold;

color: #333;

text-align: center;

padding: 10px 20px;

}

6. Avoid Global Styles

Global styles can lead to unintended consequences. Scope your styles to specific components or sections of your web page to minimize conflicts.

7. Use a CSS Preprocessor

Consider using a CSS preprocessor like SASS or LESS. They offer features like variables, nesting, and mixins, which can make your code more organized and maintainable.

8. Regularly Review and Refactor

Regular code reviews and refactoring sessions can help identify and address issues in your CSS. As your project evolves, so should your CSS.

In conclusion, writing clean and maintainable CSS involves adopting naming conventions, keeping selectors concise, using comments judiciously, grouping related properties, and following best practices. These strategies will contribute to a more efficient development process and better-maintained codebase.

Section 15.2: Organizing CSS Files and Folder Structures

One of the challenges in maintaining a large CSS codebase is keeping it organized and structured. Without a well-thought-out organization system, your CSS can quickly become unwieldy and difficult to manage. In this section, we'll explore techniques for organizing CSS files and folder structures effectively.

1. Use a Modular Approach

Modular CSS involves breaking down your styles into smaller, reusable components. Each component's styles are contained within its own CSS file or section of a CSS file. This approach makes it easier to find, update, and maintain styles for specific elements or components on your website.

2. Separate Concerns

Following the Separation of Concerns (SoC) principle is essential for maintainable CSS. It suggests keeping your HTML, CSS, and JavaScript separate. In terms of CSS, this means avoiding inline styles and keeping all your styles in external CSS files.

3. Folder Structure

Organize your CSS files into a structured folder hierarchy. A common approach is to have folders for different parts of your website, such as "layouts," "components," "utilities," and so on. Within each folder, you can further organize CSS files by function or component.

Here's an example folder structure:

styles/

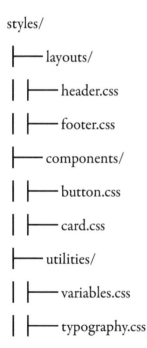

├── layouts/

│   ├── header.css

│   ├── footer.css

├── components/

│   ├── button.css

│   ├── card.css

├── utilities/

│   ├── variables.css

│   ├── typography.css

4. Modularize Component Styles

When creating component styles, consider modularization. Each component should have its own CSS file that contains styles specific to that component. This way, when you need to make changes or debug a component, you know exactly where to find its styles.

5. Use a Main Stylesheet

Create a main stylesheet (e.g., "styles.css" or "main.css") that imports all other CSS files. This file serves as the entry point for your CSS and should be linked to your HTML documents. It helps maintain a clear and organized structure for your styles.

```
/* styles.css */

@import 'layouts/header.css';

@import 'layouts/footer.css';

@import 'components/button.css';

@import 'components/card.css';

@import 'utilities/variables.css';

@import 'utilities/typography.css';
```

6. Minimize Global Scope

Avoid defining global styles that affect elements throughout your website unless absolutely necessary. Instead, scope styles to specific components or sections of your site to reduce the risk of unintended conflicts.

7. Use a Build Process

In larger projects, consider using a build process or task runner like Gulp or Webpack to compile and optimize your CSS. These tools can help concatenate and minify CSS files, making your stylesheets more efficient.

8. Version Control

Use a version control system (e.g., Git) to track changes to your CSS code. This allows you to collaborate with other developers, revert changes if needed, and maintain a history of your stylesheets.

In summary, organizing CSS files and folder structures is crucial for maintaining a scalable and maintainable codebase. By adopting a modular approach, separating concerns, structuring your folders logically, and using a main stylesheet, you can keep your CSS organized and make it easier to collaborate with other developers.

Section 15.3: BEM (Block, Element, Modifier) Methodology

When working on large and complex CSS projects, maintaining a clear and consistent naming convention for your CSS classes is essential. The BEM (Block, Element, Modifier) methodology is a popular approach that provides a structured way to name and organize CSS classes. In this section, we'll delve into the details of BEM and how to apply it effectively.

1. Understanding BEM

BEM is a naming convention that divides your CSS classes into three categories:

- **Block**: A standalone, reusable component that represents a high-level module or element on your page. Blocks are self-contained and should not depend on other blocks.

- **Element**: A part of a block that has no standalone meaning and is semantically tied to the block. Elements are typically scoped to the context of their parent block and should not be used outside of it.

- **Modifier**: A class that alters the style or behavior of a block or element. Modifiers are optional and provide a way to create variations of blocks and elements without rewriting CSS code.

2. BEM Naming Convention

The BEM naming convention follows a specific format:

- **Block**: .block-name

- **Element**: .block-name__element-name

- **Modifier**: .block-name—modifier-name

Here's a breakdown of each part:

- block-name: Represents the name of the block or component.

- element-name: Represents the name of an element within the block.

- modifier-name: Represents the name of a modifier applied to the block or element.

3. Benefits of BEM

3.1. Improved Readability

BEM class names are descriptive and self-explanatory, making it easier for developers to understand the purpose of a class without needing to inspect the CSS code.

3.2. Reduced Specificity

BEM reduces the need for deep, overly specific selectors in your CSS, which can lead to specificity conflicts and make it challenging to override styles.

3.3. Isolation

Each block or element in BEM is isolated, meaning styles defined for one block do not unintentionally affect other parts of the page. This isolation enhances maintainability.

3.4. Reusability

Blocks and elements in BEM are designed to be reusable across different parts of your website, promoting a modular and scalable codebase.

4. BEM in Practice

Here's an example of how BEM class names might be applied to an HTML structure:

```
<div class="card">
```

```html
<h2 class="card__title">Card Title</h2>
```

```html
<p class="card__text">This is some card content.</p>
```

```html
<button class="card__button card__button—primary">Primary
Button</button>
```

```html
<button                          class="card__button
card__button—secondary">Secondary Button</button>
```

```html
</div>
```

In this example:

- card is the block representing the card component.

- card__title, card__text, and card__button are elements within the card block.

- card__button—primary and card__button—secondary are modifiers that indicate different button styles.

5. Consistency is Key

To fully benefit from BEM, it's crucial to maintain consistency throughout your project. Ensure that all team members understand and follow the BEM naming convention consistently. Tools and linters can help enforce naming conventions and maintain code quality.

By adopting the BEM methodology, you can enhance the maintainability, reusability, and scalability of your CSS code, making it easier to work on large and complex projects collaboratively.

Section 15.4: CSS Comments and Documentation

Proper documentation is crucial when it comes to maintaining and collaborating on CSS code. In this section, we'll explore the importance of adding comments and documentation to your CSS files, and we'll discuss best practices for doing so.

1. The Role of CSS Comments

CSS comments are pieces of text within your CSS code that are not interpreted by the browser. They serve several essential purposes:

1.1. Explanation and Context

Comments provide context and explanations for your CSS rules, making it easier for other developers (or even your future self) to understand the purpose and functionality of specific code blocks.

1.2. Debugging

Comments can be valuable for debugging. By temporarily commenting out portions of your code, you can identify issues or isolate problematic areas without deleting the code entirely.

1.3. Collaboration

In collaborative projects, comments help team members understand the intentions behind the code. They facilitate smoother collaboration and reduce the chances of misunderstandings.

2. Best Practices for CSS Comments

When adding comments to your CSS code, consider the following best practices:

2.1. Use Descriptive Comments

Write comments that clearly explain the purpose of the code they accompany. Describe why a particular rule exists and any relevant information about its usage.

```css
/* This rule sets the background color for the header element. */

header {

background-color: #333;

}
```

2.2. Comment Sections

Organize your CSS file into sections with header comments. These sections might include headers like "Typography," "Header Styles," or "Footer Styles," making it easy to navigate and find specific rules.

```css
/* Header Styles */

.header {

/* ... */

}

/* Footer Styles */

.footer {
```

```
/*... */

}
```

2.3. Comment Dependencies

If a CSS rule depends on specific HTML structure or JavaScript functionality, mention it in the comments. This can be helpful when changes are made to related code.

```
/* Styles for the login form */

.login-form {

/*... */

}

/* Styles for the login form when the user is authenticated */

/* Depends on JS functionality to add 'authenticated' class */

.login-form.authenticated {

/*... */

}
```

2.4. Commenting Out Code

When you need to comment out a block of code temporarily, use block comments to ensure that it's clear the code is intentionally disabled.

```
/* This rule is temporarily disabled for debugging purposes */

/*
```

.example-rule {

/ ... */*

}

/

2.5. Remove Unnecessary Comments

Over time, CSS files can accumulate unnecessary comments that no longer provide value. Regularly review and remove comments that are no longer relevant to keep your codebase clean.

3. CSS Documentation Tools

Several tools can help automate the process of documenting CSS code. Popular options include:

- **Styleguides**: Create living styleguides that automatically generate documentation based on your CSS code.

- **CSS Documentation Generators**: Tools like SassDoc and PostCSS Docs can generate documentation from comments within your CSS preprocessor or postprocessor code.

- **CSS Linters**: Many CSS linters, such as Stylelint, can enforce consistent commenting and documentation practices.

By following these best practices and using appropriate documentation tools, you can maintain well-structured and well-documented CSS code, which is essential for efficient development and collaboration.

Section 15.5: Version Control for CSS

Version control is a crucial aspect of modern software development, including web development with CSS. In this section, we'll explore why version control is essential for CSS, how to set up version control for your CSS projects, and best practices for using version control effectively.

1. The Importance of Version Control

Version control systems (VCS), such as Git, provide several advantages for managing CSS and web development projects:

1.1. Collaboration

Version control allows multiple developers to work on the same CSS codebase simultaneously without conflicts. Each developer can create their branch to work on features or fixes independently.

1.2. History and Rollbacks

VCS tracks changes made to CSS files, creating a history of revisions. This history is invaluable for debugging, identifying when issues were introduced, and rolling back to previous, stable versions.

1.3. Code Reviews

VCS enables code reviews, allowing team members to review and comment on each other's CSS code before merging changes into the main codebase.

1.4. Backup and Recovery

CSS code stored in a version control system serves as a backup. Even if a local copy is lost or corrupted, the code can be retrieved from the repository.

2. Setting Up Version Control

To get started with version control for your CSS projects, follow these steps:

2.1. Install Git

If you haven't already, install Git on your development machine. You can download Git from the official website (https://git-scm.com/downloads) and follow the installation instructions for your operating system.

2.2. Initialize a Git Repository

Navigate to your CSS project directory using your terminal or command prompt and run the following command to initialize a Git repository:

git init

2.3. Create a .gitignore File

To prevent specific files and directories (e.g., compiled CSS files or temporary build directories) from being tracked by Git, create a .gitignore file in your project's root directory and list the files and patterns to ignore. For example:

Ignore compiled CSS files

*.css

Ignore build directories

/build/

2.4. Add and Commit Changes

After making changes to your CSS files, add them to the staging area using the git add command and commit your changes with a meaningful message:

git add .

git commit -m "Added responsive styles for mobile devices"

2.5. Create Branches

For collaborative work or when working on specific features or bug fixes, create branches using the git branch and git checkout commands. For example, to create and switch to a new branch:

git branch feature-navigation

git checkout feature-navigation

3. Best Practices for Version Control

To make the most of version control for CSS development, consider these best practices:

3.1. Use Meaningful Commit Messages

Write clear and descriptive commit messages that summarize the purpose of each change. This helps team members understand the context of your commits.

3.2. Frequent Commits

Commit your changes frequently, keeping each commit focused on a single task or improvement. Avoid creating overly large commits with unrelated changes.

3.3. Regularly Pull and Push

Fetch and merge changes from the remote repository using git pull to keep your local copy up-to-date. Push your changes to the remote repository to share them with your team.

3.4. Branch Strategy

Use branches for different tasks or features. Consider adopting a branch naming convention to make it easier to identify the purpose of each branch.

3.5. Code Reviews

Leverage pull requests or merge requests for code reviews before merging changes into the main branch. This helps maintain code quality and consistency.

3.6. *Continuous Integration (CI)*

Integrate version control with CI tools to automate testing and deployment processes. This ensures that changes to your CSS code are thoroughly tested before being deployed to production.

By implementing version control and following these best practices, you'll enhance collaboration, code quality, and the overall development process for your CSS projects.

Chapter 16: CSS Grid Frameworks and Systems

In this chapter, we'll delve into the world of CSS grid frameworks and systems. These tools and methodologies help web developers create consistent and responsive layouts quickly and efficiently.

Section 16.1: Overview of CSS Grid Frameworks

CSS grid frameworks are pre-built systems that simplify layout design, making it easier to create complex grid-based designs. They provide a set of predefined classes, styles, and layout components that you can use in your projects. Let's explore the key aspects of CSS grid frameworks.

1. What Are CSS Grid Frameworks?

CSS grid frameworks are collections of CSS rules and classes designed to streamline the creation of grid-based layouts. They offer a consistent grid structure, typography, and utility classes, making it easier to achieve responsive and aesthetically pleasing designs.

2. Advantages of CSS Grid Frameworks

2.1. Rapid Development

CSS grid frameworks accelerate the development process by providing ready-made components and styles. Developers can focus on content and functionality rather than spending time on layout design.

2.2. Consistency

Frameworks ensure design consistency across projects and teams. By adhering to predefined classes and guidelines, developers maintain a cohesive look and feel.

2.3. Responsive Design

Many CSS grid frameworks are inherently responsive, meaning they adapt to different screen sizes and devices. This is essential for modern web design.

2.4. Grid Systems

Grid frameworks offer grid systems with predefined column structures. Developers can easily create multi-column layouts for various content types.

3. Popular CSS Grid Frameworks

3.1. Bootstrap

Bootstrap is one of the most widely used CSS grid frameworks. It provides a comprehensive set of styles, components, and responsive grid classes. Bootstrap's grid system is based on a 12-column layout, making it highly flexible.

3.2. Foundation

Foundation is another popular framework known for its mobile-first approach. It offers a robust grid system, UI components, and a wide range of customization options.

3.3. Bulma

Bulma is a modern CSS framework that focuses on simplicity and flexibility. It provides a clean grid system and numerous utility classes.

3.4. Materialize

Materialize is a framework that implements Google's Material Design principles. It offers a grid system, CSS components, and JavaScript features for building modern web applications.

4. Choosing the Right Framework

When selecting a CSS grid framework, consider factors like project requirements, design preferences, and ease of customization. Different frameworks have their own strengths and weaknesses, so choose one that aligns with your specific needs.

5. Custom Grid Design

While CSS grid frameworks are convenient, some projects may benefit from a custom grid design tailored to unique requirements. In such cases, CSS Grid Layout (not to be confused with frameworks) offers complete control over grid structures and responsiveness.

In the following sections, we will explore specific CSS grid frameworks in more detail and learn how to implement them in your projects. Whether you opt for a popular framework like Bootstrap or decide to create a custom grid, mastering CSS grid systems is essential for modern web development.

Section 16.2: Grid Systems for Layout Consistency

In this section, we'll delve deeper into the concept of grid systems and their role in maintaining layout consistency across web projects. Grid systems are a fundamental aspect of CSS grid frameworks and play a crucial role in achieving visually pleasing and organized designs.

1. Understanding Grid Systems

A grid system is a set of guidelines and rules that define the structure of a layout. It consists of rows and columns that create a framework for organizing content. Grid systems are used to establish a consistent and balanced arrangement of elements on a web page.

2. Key Components of a Grid System

2.1. Rows

Rows are horizontal divisions within a grid system. They serve as containers for content and are usually separated by gutters (empty spaces). Rows ensure that content is organized vertically.

2.2. Columns

Columns are vertical divisions within a grid system. They define the width of content blocks. A grid typically has a fixed number of columns, and content elements span one or more columns.

2.3. Gutters

Gutters are the spaces between rows and columns. They provide visual separation and spacing between content elements. Gutters contribute to the overall readability and aesthetics of the layout.

3. Advantages of Grid Systems

3.1. Consistency

Grid systems enforce consistency by defining a predictable structure for layout elements. Elements align with grid lines, creating a cohesive design.

3.2. Responsiveness

Grid systems can be designed to adapt to different screen sizes and devices. This responsiveness is essential for modern web design, as it ensures a seamless user experience across platforms.

3.3. Ease of Alignment

Grid systems make it easier to align elements both vertically and horizontally. Elements snap to the grid, eliminating the need for manual adjustments.

3.4. Efficient Design

Developers and designers can work more efficiently with grid systems. Content placement becomes systematic, reducing the time required for layout design.

4. Grid Systems in CSS Grid Frameworks

CSS grid frameworks, like Bootstrap and Foundation, incorporate grid systems as a core feature. They provide predefined classes for creating rows, columns, and gutters. Developers can simply apply these classes to HTML elements to establish a consistent grid-based layout.

5. Custom Grid Systems

In some cases, projects may require custom grid systems tailored to specific design needs. CSS Grid Layout is a powerful tool for creating custom grid systems. It offers complete control over grid structure, making it suitable for unique layouts that don't fit the constraints of predefined frameworks.

6. Implementing Grid Systems

To implement a grid system in your project, you'll typically include the relevant CSS classes or styles provided by the chosen framework. These classes define the grid's properties, such as the number of columns, gutter width, and responsiveness breakpoints.

In the next section, we'll explore how to create grid-based layouts using a popular CSS grid framework, providing hands-on examples and practical guidance. Understanding grid systems and their implementation is crucial for achieving layout consistency and design flexibility in web development.

Section 16.3: Custom Grid Design with CSS Grid

In this section, we will explore the versatility and power of CSS Grid Layout for creating custom grid systems. While CSS frameworks offer predefined grid structures, there are cases where you need to design unique layouts tailored to specific project requirements. CSS Grid allows you to create highly customized grid systems from scratch.

1. CSS Grid Overview

CSS Grid Layout is a two-dimensional layout system that provides precise control over rows and columns. It enables you to define both the size and placement of grid items within a grid container. To create a custom grid, follow these steps:

2. Define a Grid Container

First, designate an HTML element as your grid container. This element will contain the grid items. Apply the following CSS property to define it as a grid container:

.container {

display: grid;

}

3. Define Rows and Columns

Specify the structure of your grid by defining rows and columns. You can use various units of measurement (e.g., pixels, percentages, or fr units) to determine their size. For example:

.container {

display: grid;

grid-template-rows: repeat(3, 1fr); /* *Three rows with equal height* */

grid-template-columns: 1fr 2fr 1fr; /* *Three columns with varying width* */

}

4. Place Grid Items

Now, place your content elements within the grid by specifying their position in terms of grid row and column lines. You can use the grid-row and grid-column properties to achieve this:

.item1 {

grid-row: 1 / 2; /* *Start on row line 1 and end on row line 2* */

grid-column: 1 / 4; /* *Start on column line 1 and end on column line 4* */

}

5. Additional Grid Properties

CSS Grid provides additional properties for controlling the behavior of your grid, such as:

- grid-gap: Defines the spacing between grid items.

- grid-template-areas: Assigns names to areas within the grid, making it easy to place items.

- grid-auto-rows and grid-auto-columns: Define default sizes for rows and columns not explicitly specified.

6. Grid Responsiveness

To make your custom grid responsive, use media queries to adjust the grid's structure based on screen size. For instance, you can change the number of columns or their widths for smaller screens.

@media screen and (max-width: 768px) {

.container {

grid-template-columns: 1fr; /* Single column layout for small screens */

}

}

7. Benefits of Custom Grids

Custom grids offer complete design flexibility, allowing you to create unique and visually appealing layouts. They are particularly useful when your project demands unconventional designs that can't be achieved with standard grid frameworks.

8. Case Studies

In this section, we will present practical case studies demonstrating the creation of custom grid layouts using CSS Grid. These examples will illustrate how to design grids for various types of content and responsiveness requirements.

Custom grid design with CSS Grid empowers you to take full control of your layout, ensuring that your web projects stand out with distinctive and user-friendly designs.

Section 16.4: Implementing Grid Systems

Responsively

Creating responsive grid systems is essential for ensuring that your web designs adapt to various screen sizes and devices. In this section, we'll explore how to implement responsive grid systems effectively using CSS Grid.

1. Media Queries for Responsive Grids

To make your grid layouts responsive, you'll need to use CSS media queries. Media queries allow you to apply different CSS rules based on the user's device or screen size. Here's an example of how you can adjust a grid's layout for different screen widths:

/* *Define a grid with two columns for screens wider than 768px* */

.container {

display: grid;

grid-template-columns: repeat(2, 1fr);

}

/* *Adjust the grid to a single column for screens 768px or narrower* */

@media screen **and** (**max-width**: 768px) {

.container {

grid-template-columns: 1fr;

}

}

In this example, when the screen width is 768 pixels or less, the grid changes from a two-column layout to a single-column layout.

2. Fluid Grids with Fractional Units (fr)

CSS Grid's fractional unit (fr) is a valuable tool for creating fluid grid systems. You can use fr units to distribute available space among grid columns or rows. Here's an example:

.container {

display: grid;

grid-template-columns: 1fr 2fr; /* *First column gets 1/3, second column gets 2/3 of available width* */

}

This approach ensures that columns adapt proportionally to the available space, making your grid responsive by design.

3. Auto-Sizing Grid Items

CSS Grid allows grid items to automatically size themselves based on their content or the available space within a grid cell. This can simplify responsive design. For instance, you can create responsive grids where items grow or shrink based on content or screen size without explicit column definitions:

.container {

display: grid;

grid-template-columns: repeat(auto-fill, minmax(200px, 1fr));

}

In this example, the auto-fill keyword creates as many columns as will fit in the container, each with a minimum width of 200px and a maximum width that takes up the available space evenly.

4. Controlling Grid Item Placement

CSS Grid provides control over where grid items are placed within the grid. You can use media queries to adjust placement as needed. For example:

.item {

grid-column: span 2; /* *Item spans 2 columns by default* */

}

@media screen **and** (**max-width**: 768px) {

.item {

grid-column: span 1; /* *Item spans 1 column on smaller screens* */

}

}

This code ensures that the grid item spans two columns on wider screens but only one column on screens with a maximum width of 768 pixels.

5. Testing Across Devices

Testing is crucial when implementing responsive grid systems. Use browser developer tools to preview your design across various devices and screen sizes. Ensure that your grid adapts smoothly to different viewports and maintains readability and usability.

By effectively using media queries, fractional units, and auto-sizing, you can create responsive grid systems that deliver a seamless user experience across a wide range of devices and screen sizes. These techniques provide the flexibility needed to design grids that look and function well on desktops, tablets, and mobile devices.

Section 16.5: Case Studies: Grid Systems in Action

In this section, we'll delve into practical case studies that showcase the implementation of grid systems using CSS Grid in real-world scenarios. These examples will help you understand how to apply grid layouts to various types of web designs effectively.

1. Portfolio Website Layout

Suppose you're designing a portfolio website with a responsive grid layout to showcase your projects. You can create a grid structure where each project item is evenly distributed across the screen, adapting to different screen sizes.

.project-grid {

display: grid;

grid-template-columns: repeat(auto-fill, minmax(300px, 1fr));

gap: 20px;

}

In this example, the auto-fill keyword generates as many columns as possible while ensuring that each column is at least 300px wide. The gap property adds spacing between the project items.

2. E-Commerce Product Listings

For an e-commerce website, you can use CSS Grid to display product listings in a grid format. This layout allows for easy scanning of products while ensuring a consistent and visually appealing design.

.product-grid {

display: grid;

grid-template-columns: repeat(auto-fill, minmax(200px, 1fr));

gap: 10px;

}

Here, the grid adapts to the available space, with each column being at least 200px wide and adjusting based on the screen size. The gap property provides spacing between product items.

3. Magazine-Style Blog Layout

Creating a magazine-style blog layout often requires a grid system to arrange articles in an organized and visually appealing manner. CSS Grid simplifies this task:

.blog-grid {

display: grid;

grid-template-columns: 2fr 1fr;

gap: 20px;

}

In this example, the layout consists of two columns where the main content occupies two-thirds of the width, and the sidebar takes up one-third. The gap property adds spacing between content sections.

4. Responsive Dashboard Design

Dashboards often feature multiple panels with varying content. CSS Grid can be used to create a responsive dashboard layout that reorganizes panels based on screen size:

```
.dashboard-grid {

display: grid;

grid-template-columns: repeat(auto-fit, minmax(300px, 1fr));

gap: 15px;

}
```

This grid layout ensures that panels are evenly distributed across the screen, with each panel being at least 300px wide but adapting to the available space.

5. Event Calendar Display

For event calendar displays, CSS Grid can be utilized to arrange events in a calendar-like grid. Here's an example:

```
.calendar-grid {

display: grid;

grid-template-columns: repeat(7, 1fr);

gap: 10px;

}
```

In this grid, each column represents a day of the week, allowing for a structured presentation of events. The gap property adds spacing between calendar items.

These case studies demonstrate the versatility of CSS Grid in handling a wide range of layout requirements. By customizing grid properties and leveraging media queries, you can create responsive and visually appealing web designs tailored to your specific project's needs. Whether you're building a portfolio, an e-commerce site, a blog, a dashboard, or an event calendar, CSS Grid provides the flexibility to implement grid systems that enhance user experience and visual aesthetics.

Chapter 17: Design Trends and CSS

Section 17.1: Current Web Design Trends

Web design is an ever-evolving field, with design trends constantly changing to meet the needs and preferences of users. Staying up-to-date with the latest design trends and incorporating them into your CSS styles can give your websites a fresh and modern look. In this section, we'll explore some of the current web design trends and how you can use CSS to implement them effectively.

1. Minimalism and White Space

Minimalism remains a strong design trend. It focuses on simplicity, using clean layouts and generous white space. CSS can help achieve this by using minimalistic fonts, clean lines, and uncluttered designs. Here's an example of CSS for a minimalistic layout:

body {

font-family: 'Helvetica Neue', sans-serif;

background-color: #fff;

color: #333;

margin: 0;

padding: 0;

line-height: 1.6;

}

.container {

```
max-width: 1200px;

margin: 0 auto;

padding: 20px;

}
```

2. Dark Mode

Dark mode has gained popularity due to its visual appeal and reduced eye strain. CSS allows you to implement dark mode easily by defining different color schemes for light and dark themes. Here's an example of CSS for dark mode:

```
body {

background-color: #333;

color: #fff;

}

.button {

background-color: #555;

color: #fff;

}
```

3. Bold Typography

Using bold and expressive typography is a trend that can make your content stand out. CSS custom fonts and text effects can be applied to create striking typography:

```
h1 {
```

font-family: 'Poppins', sans-serif;

font-weight: 700;

font-size: 36px;

color: #333;

text-transform: uppercase;

letter-spacing: 2px;

}

4. Gradient Backgrounds

Gradients add depth and dimension to web designs. CSS gradients can be easily applied to elements:

.button {

background: linear-gradient(135deg, #ff6a00, #ee0979);

color: #fff;

}

5. Microinteractions

Microinteractions, such as subtle hover effects and animations, enhance user engagement. CSS animations and transitions can create these effects:

.button {

transition: background-color 0.3s ease;

}

```
.button:hover {

background-color: #ff6a00;

}
```

6. Illustrations and Custom Graphics

Custom graphics and illustrations can make your website unique. CSS can be used for positioning and styling custom graphics:

```
.illustration {

background-image: url('illustration.png');

background-size: cover;

width: 100%;

height: 300px;

}
```

7. Responsive Typography

Responsive typography ensures that text scales appropriately across different screen sizes. CSS media queries can be used to adjust font sizes:

```
@media (max-width: 768px) {

h1 {

font-size: 24px;

}

}
```

These are just a few of the current web design trends that you can implement using CSS. Staying informed about design trends and applying them with CSS can help you create websites that are not only visually appealing but also user-friendly and up-to-date with the latest industry standards.

Section 17.2: Applying Design Trends with CSS

In the ever-evolving world of web design, it's essential to stay updated with the latest trends and adapt your CSS styles accordingly. In the previous section, we discussed some current design trends. Now, let's explore how to apply these trends effectively using CSS.

1. Implementing Responsive Design

Responsive web design is not just a trend but a fundamental necessity. CSS plays a pivotal role in making your designs responsive. Using media queries, you can adjust the layout and styling of your website based on the user's device or screen size. Here's an example of a simple media query to make a website responsive:

```
/* Base styles for desktop */

.header {

font-size: 24px;

}

/* Responsive styles for mobile devices */

@media (max-width: 768px) {

.header {
```

```
font-size: 18px;

}

}
```

2. Customizing Color Schemes

Adapting your color scheme to current trends can significantly impact the visual appeal of your website. CSS makes it easy to customize colors throughout your site. For example, you can use CSS variables (custom properties) to define a color scheme and apply it consistently:

```
:root {

—primary-color: #007bff;

—secondary-color: #ff6a00;

}
.button {

background-color: var(—primary-color);

color: #fff;

}
.button:hover {

background-color: var(—secondary-color);

}
```

3. Typography Enhancements

Bold typography is a prevalent trend in modern web design. You can leverage CSS to make your text more expressive. Use custom fonts and adjust text properties like font weight, size, and letter spacing:

body {

font-family: 'Montserrat', sans-serif;

}

h1 {

font-weight: 700;

font-size: 36px;

letter-spacing: 1px;

}

4. Creating Engaging Microinteractions

Microinteractions are subtle animations or effects that engage users. CSS animations and transitions are perfect for implementing microinteractions. For instance, you can create a smooth hover effect for buttons:

.button {

transition: transform 0.3s ease;

}

.button:*hover* {

transform: scale(1.1);

}

5. Optimizing for Dark Mode

Dark mode is a user-friendly trend. CSS makes it simple to provide a dark mode option on your website. Define dark mode styles and toggle them based on user preferences or system settings:

/* Light mode styles */

body {

background-color: #fff;

color: #333;

}

/* Dark mode styles */

.dark-mode body {

background-color: #333;

color: #fff;

}

6. Utilizing Gradients

Gradients can add depth to your designs. CSS allows you to create gradients easily. For example, you can apply a gradient background to elements like buttons:

.button {

background: linear-gradient(135deg, #ff6a00, #ee0979);

color: #fff;

}

7. Incorporating Custom Graphics

Custom graphics and illustrations can make your site unique. CSS positioning and styling can be used to integrate custom graphics seamlessly:

.illustration {

background-image: url('illustration.png');

background-size: cover;

width: 100%;

height: 300px;

}

By understanding how to apply these design trends using CSS, you can create websites that are not only visually appealing but also in line with the latest industry standards. Keep experimenting with CSS to achieve the desired aesthetics and user experience.

Section 17.3: Responsive Typography and Color Schemes

In the world of web design, creating responsive and visually appealing websites is essential. Two key aspects that greatly contribute to the overall aesthetics and usability of a website are typography and color schemes. In this section, we'll explore the importance of responsive typography and color schemes and how CSS can be leveraged to achieve these design goals effectively.

Responsive Typography

Typography plays a crucial role in conveying information and setting the tone for your website. With the increasing variety of devices and screen sizes, it's vital to ensure that your typography is responsive and legible across all platforms.

Using Relative Units

One way to make typography responsive is by using relative units such as em and rem. These units allow font sizes to scale based on the parent element's font size, making it easier to maintain a consistent typographic hierarchy.

body {

font-size: 16px; /* *Set a base font size* */

}

h1 {

font-size: 2rem; /* *Relative to the base font size (32px)* */

}

p {

font-size: 1rem; /* *Relative to the base font size (16px)* */

}

@media (**max-width**: 768px) {

body {

font-size: 14px; /* *Adjust the base font size for smaller screens* */

```
}
```

```
}
```

Fluid Typography

Another approach is to implement fluid typography, where font sizes adjust smoothly as the viewport size changes. CSS variables (custom properties) can be utilized for this purpose:

```
:root {
```

```
—base-font-size: 16px;
```

```
—font-scale-factor: 0.5vw; /* Adjust the scaling factor as needed */
```

```
}
```

```
body {
```

```
font-size: var(—base-font-size);
```

```
}
```

```
h1 {
```

```
font-size: calc(var(—base-font-size) + var(—font-scale-factor) * 6);
```

```
}
```

```
p {
```

```
font-size: calc(var(—base-font-size) + var(—font-scale-factor) * 2);
```

```
}
```

Color Schemes

Color schemes greatly impact a website's visual appeal and user experience. Creating responsive color schemes ensures that your site maintains its aesthetics on various devices.

Using CSS Variables for Color

CSS variables (custom properties) are invaluable for defining and maintaining consistent color schemes throughout your website. They can be easily updated to accommodate different color variations:

:root {

—primary-color: #007bff;

—secondary-color: #ff6a00;

}

.button {

background-color: var(—primary-color);

color: #fff;

}

.button:*hover* {

background-color: var(—secondary-color);

}

Dark Mode Support

Supporting dark mode has become a design trend and accessibility feature. CSS allows you to create a dark mode version of your site by defining alternate styles and toggling them based on user preferences or system settings:

```
/* Light mode styles */

body {

background-color: #fff;

color: #333;

}

/* Dark mode styles */

.dark-mode body {

background-color: #333;

color: #fff;

}
```

In conclusion, responsive typography and color schemes are vital components of modern web design. CSS provides the necessary tools and techniques to ensure that your website's typography is legible and visually appealing across various devices while also maintaining consistent and adaptable color schemes. By mastering these aspects, you can create websites that engage users and provide an excellent user experience.

Section 17.4: Exploring Microinteractions

Microinteractions are subtle, functional animations and feedback that occur within a user interface. They can enhance the user experience by providing feedback, guiding users, and making interactions more engaging. In this section, we'll delve into the world of microinteractions and how they can be implemented using CSS and JavaScript.

Understanding Microinteractions

Microinteractions are the small details that users may not consciously notice but greatly impact their interaction with a website or app. These interactions can include animations for button clicks, form validation, hover effects, and more.

Creating Microinteractions with CSS

CSS animations and transitions are powerful tools for creating microinteractions without the need for JavaScript. Let's look at an example of how you can add a smooth hover effect to a button:

.button {

background-color: #007bff;

color: #fff;

padding: 10px 20px;

border: none;

cursor: pointer;

transition: background-color 0.3s ease;

}

```css
.button:hover {

background-color: #0056b3;

}
```

In this example, when a user hovers over the button, the background color smoothly transitions to a darker shade, providing visual feedback.

Adding Microinteractions with JavaScript

For more complex microinteractions, JavaScript can be used to control animations and interactions. Let's consider a scenario where you want to create a microinteraction for a toggle switch:

```html
<label class="toggle-switch">

<input type="checkbox" id="toggle" />

<span class="slider"></span>

</label>
```

```css
.toggle-switch {

position: relative;

display: inline-block;

width: 60px;

height: 34px;

}

.toggle-switch input[type="checkbox"] {

display: none;
```

```css
}
.slider {
position: absolute;
cursor: pointer;
top: 0;
left: 0;
right: 0;
bottom: 0;
background-color: #ccc;
transition: 0.4s;
border-radius: 34px;
}
.slider:before {
position: absolute;
content: "";
height: 26px;
width: 26px;
left: 4px;
bottom: 4px;
background-color: white;
```

```
transition: 0.4s;

border-radius: 50%;

}

input[type="checkbox"]:checked + .slider {

background-color: #2196F3;

}

input[type="checkbox"]:checked + .slider:before {

transform: translateX(26px);

}
```

In this example, we use JavaScript to create a custom toggle switch with a sliding animation. When the checkbox is checked, the slider moves to the right, changing the background color. This is a more complex microinteraction that enhances user engagement.

Microinteractions for User Feedback

Microinteractions are also valuable for providing feedback to users. For instance, you can use them to validate form input and display error messages or confirmations without overwhelming the user with a large dialog box. By using subtle animations or changes in color, you can guide users through their interactions and make the overall experience more intuitive.

In conclusion, microinteractions are an essential aspect of modern web design. They add depth and engagement to user interfaces, making interactions more enjoyable and informative. Whether using CSS or JavaScript, mastering microinteractions can greatly enhance the user experience on your website or web application.

Section 17.5: Future Trends in CSS Styling

As the field of web development evolves, so does the landscape of CSS styling. In this section, we'll explore some future trends and emerging practices in CSS that are likely to shape the way we design and style web applications and websites in the coming years.

1. CSS Variables (Custom Properties)

CSS Custom Properties, often referred to as CSS variables, have gained widespread adoption in recent years. They allow developers to define reusable values within CSS files, promoting modularity and easier theming of web applications. With CSS variables, you can create dynamic and consistent designs by centralizing color schemes, typography, and other design variables. This trend is likely to continue as developers harness the power of custom properties to build more maintainable and flexible stylesheets.

:root {

—primary-color: #007bff;

—secondary-color: #0056b3;

}

.button {

background-color: var(—primary-color);

color: #fff;

padding: 10px 20px;

}

2. CSS-in-JS and Styled Components

CSS-in-JS is an emerging trend that involves writing CSS styles directly in JavaScript files. Libraries like Styled Components and Emotion have gained popularity for their ability to encapsulate styles within React components, improving component-based styling and reducing global CSS conflicts. This approach provides more predictability and maintainability in complex web applications.

```
import styled from 'styled-components';

const Button = styled.button`

background-color: #007bff;

color: #fff;

padding: 10px 20px;

`;
```

3. Dark Mode and Theming

With the increasing demand for dark mode and theming options in web applications, CSS is evolving to accommodate these preferences. Media queries and CSS variables make it easier to implement dynamic themes that adapt to user preferences. Additionally, newer CSS features like the prefers-color-scheme media query enable automatic switching between light and dark modes based on the user's system preferences.

```
@media (prefers-color-scheme: dark) {

/* Dark mode styles here */

}
```

4. CSS Houdini

CSS Houdini is an exciting development that aims to give developers more control over the CSS rendering engine. It allows developers to create custom CSS properties, values, and animations, opening up new possibilities for creative and efficient styling. As browser support for CSS Houdini expands, we can expect to see innovative and performance-enhancing styles in web applications.

5. Container Queries

Container queries are another upcoming CSS feature that will allow styles to adapt based on the dimensions of a container, rather than just the viewport. This feature is particularly useful for creating responsive components that adjust to their parent containers, making it easier to design flexible layouts.

```css
.container {

width: 100%;

}
/* Styles that adapt to the container width */
```

6. 3D and Spatial CSS

With the increasing popularity of augmented reality (AR) and virtual reality (VR) experiences on the web, 3D and spatial CSS is becoming more relevant. CSS features like 3D transforms, animations, and VR-related properties will play a significant role in shaping immersive web experiences.

```css
.card {

transform: translateZ(50px);
```

```
animation: spin 2s infinite linear;

}

@keyframes spin {

from {

transform: rotate(0deg);

}

to {

transform: rotate(360deg);

}

}
```

In conclusion, CSS continues to evolve, and web developers must stay updated with these emerging trends and features to create modern and engaging web applications. Whether it's using CSS variables for theming, adopting CSS-in-JS for better component-based styling, or exploring the possibilities of CSS Houdini, the future of CSS promises exciting opportunities for web design and development.

Chapter 18: Internationalization and Localization

Section 18.1: CSS for Multilingual Websites

In our increasingly interconnected world, it's essential for websites to be accessible and user-friendly for people from diverse linguistic and cultural backgrounds. Internationalization (i18n) and localization (l10n) are the processes that enable websites and applications to adapt to different languages, regions, and cultures. While most of the focus in i18n and l10n is on content and text, CSS also plays a crucial role in creating a seamless and culturally appropriate user experience. In this section, we'll explore how CSS can be used to enhance the internationalization and localization of web interfaces, specifically focusing on multilingual websites.

1. Font Selection for Multilingual Text

One of the fundamental aspects of designing a multilingual website is choosing appropriate fonts that support a wide range of scripts and characters. Some fonts are better equipped to handle multiple languages, while others may be limited in their character support. CSS allows you to define font stacks that prioritize fonts with broader character coverage.

body {

font-family: Arial, Helvetica, sans-serif;

}

2. Text Direction

Different languages are written from left to right (LTR), right to left (RTL), or even top to bottom. CSS provides the direction property to control text direction, ensuring that content flows correctly for languages with different writing systems.

```css
/* LTR direction */
p {
direction: ltr;
}
/* RTL direction */
blockquote {
direction: rtl;
}
```

3. Handling Text Overflow

Languages like German or Finnish often have longer words than English, which can lead to text overflow issues if not handled properly. CSS properties like overflow and text-overflow can be used to manage text overflow in multilingual content.

```css
/* Overflow handling */
.long-text {
white-space: nowrap;
overflow: hidden;
```

text-overflow: ellipsis;

}

4. Adjusting Line Height and Line Breaks

Different languages may require adjustments to line height and line breaks to ensure readability and aesthetics. CSS properties like line-height and word-wrap can be used for fine-tuning text layout.

/ Line height adjustment */*

h1 {

line-height: 1.5;

}

/ Word wrapping */*

.wrapped-text {

word-wrap: break-word;

}

5. Localization-Friendly Styling

When using CSS for styling, be mindful of text expansion and contraction due to translation. Avoid fixed widths and heights for elements that contain text, as they may not accommodate longer or shorter translations. Instead, use relative units like percentages or em to allow content to adapt to different text lengths.

/ Avoid fixed widths */*

.button {

```
width: 200px; /* Avoid this */

}

/* Use relative units */

.button {

width: 100%; /* Better for multilingual content */

}
```

6. Language-Specific Styling

In some cases, you may want to apply specific styles based on the language of the content. CSS provides the :lang pseudo-class to target elements with specific language attributes.

```
/* Styling for English text */

p:lang(en) {

color: #007bff;

}
/* Styling for Spanish text */

p:lang(es) {

color: #e74c3c;

}
```

In conclusion, CSS is a valuable tool for creating internationalized and localized web interfaces that cater to a global audience. When designing for multilingual websites, consider typography, text direction, text overflow, line height, and language-specific styling to ensure a seamless user experience across different languages and cultures. By incorporating these CSS techniques, you can make your website more inclusive and accessible to users worldwide.

Section 18.2: Text Direction and Language Support

In the realm of internationalization and localization (i18n and l10n), understanding and correctly implementing text direction and language support are essential. Different languages are written in various scripts, and these scripts may require different text directionality (left-to-right, right-to-left, or even top-to-bottom). Additionally, each language may have specific typographic conventions and nuances that should be considered in web design. In this section, we'll delve into the importance of text direction and language support in CSS for creating multilingual websites.

1. Defining Text Direction

One of the most critical aspects of accommodating different languages is managing text direction. Some languages, such as English, are written from left to right (LTR), while others, like Arabic or Hebrew, follow a right-to-left (RTL) direction. CSS provides the direction property to control text direction.

```
/* LTR direction */

p {

direction: ltr;

}

/* RTL direction */
```

```
blockquote {

direction: rtl;

}
```

By correctly setting the text direction, you ensure that the content is displayed in a way that respects the writing system of the language. This is crucial for readability and user experience.

2. Handling Bidirectional Text

Many multilingual websites contain content in both LTR and RTL languages. When mixing text from different directions, it's essential to manage bidirectional text correctly. CSS introduces the unicode-bidi property, which can be used in combination with direction to handle bidirectional text.

```
/* Bi-directional text */

div {

direction: rtl; /* Set overall text direction */

unicode-bidi: embed; /* Embed LTR text within RTL text */

}
```

This combination ensures that text flows correctly even when LTR and RTL languages are used together.

3. Language-specific Styling

CSS allows you to apply language-specific styling to elements based on the language attributes in your content. The :lang pseudo-class can be used to target elements with specific language attributes.

```
/* Styling for English text */
p:lang(en) {
color: #007bff;
}
/* Styling for Arabic text */
p:lang(ar) {
color: #e74c3c;
}
```

This feature enables you to adapt the visual appearance of your website to suit different languages or regions.

4. Font Selection

Different scripts may require specific fonts to be legible. When designing for multilingual websites, it's crucial to select fonts that support the character sets of the languages you intend to use. CSS allows you to define font stacks that prioritize fonts with broader character coverage.

```
body {
font-family: Arial, Helvetica, sans-serif;
}
```

In conclusion, text direction and language support are fundamental considerations when designing multilingual websites. Correctly setting text direction, handling bidirectional text, using language-specific styling, and choosing appropriate fonts are all key aspects of ensuring an effective and culturally sensitive user experience. By leveraging CSS for these purposes, you can create web interfaces that are accessible and inclusive for users from diverse linguistic backgrounds.

Section 18.3: Handling Date and Time Formats

When designing websites with internationalization and localization in mind, one crucial aspect to consider is how date and time information is presented to users. Different regions and cultures may have distinct preferences for date and time formats, and it's essential to accommodate these variations to provide a seamless user experience. In this section, we'll explore how CSS can be used to handle date and time formats on multilingual websites.

1. The Importance of Date and Time Localization

Date and time information is prevalent on websites, from event listings to blog posts. Users expect to see dates and times presented in a format that is familiar and relevant to their region. For example, in the United States, the date might be displayed as "MM/DD/YYYY," while in many European countries, it is presented as "DD/MM/YYYY." Similarly, time formats can vary from the 12-hour clock to the 24-hour clock.

2. Leveraging CSS for Date and Time Formatting

While CSS itself does not provide extensive capabilities for date and time formatting, it can be used in conjunction with HTML attributes and JavaScript to achieve localized date and time presentation. Here's how you can use CSS to style date and time elements:

```
<p class="date">October 25, 2023</p>
```

```
<p class="time">14:30</p>
```

```
/* Styling date and time elements */
```

```
.date {
```

```
font-weight: bold;
```

```
color: #007bff;
```

```
}
```

```
.time {
```

```
font-family: Arial, Helvetica, sans-serif;
```

```
font-size: 1.2rem;
```

```
color: #333;
```

```
}
```

CSS is effective for styling date and time elements to match the overall design of your website. However, for actual date and time formatting, you'll typically rely on JavaScript or server-side solutions.

3. JavaScript for Date and Time Localization

To achieve date and time localization in a dynamic way, JavaScript is often used. JavaScript provides the Date object, which can be used to format dates and times based on the user's locale. Libraries like moment.js or the built-in Intl.DateTimeFormat provide robust tools for date and time localization.

```
// Using Intl.DateTimeFormat for date formatting
```

```
const date = new Date('2023-10-25');

const dateFormatter = new Intl.DateTimeFormat('en-US', { dateStyle: 'full' });

const formattedDate = dateFormatter.format(date);

// Using moment.js for date and time formatting

const moment = require('moment');

const date = moment('2023-10-25');

const formattedDate = date.format('LLLL');
```

These JavaScript solutions allow you to format date and time information dynamically based on the user's locale and preferences.

4. Server-Side Date and Time Formatting

For server-generated content, it's common to handle date and time formatting on the server side. Server-side programming languages like PHP, Python, or Ruby offer libraries and functions for date and time localization. This ensures that the date and time formats are consistent across the entire website.

5. User Preference Considerations

In some cases, you may want to allow users to specify their preferred date and time formats. You can achieve this by providing options in your website's settings or user profile. Remember to save user preferences and apply them consistently throughout the site.

In conclusion, handling date and time formats is an integral part of creating a multilingual and globally accessible website. While CSS plays a role in styling date and time elements, the actual localization of date and time information is typically achieved through JavaScript or server-side programming. By considering the preferences of your target audience and providing flexible formatting options, you can enhance the user experience and make your website more inclusive for users from diverse cultural backgrounds.

Section 18.4: Currency and Number Formatting

Formatting numbers and currencies correctly is essential when designing internationalized websites. Different regions and cultures have distinct preferences for how numbers and currencies should be presented. In this section, we'll explore how CSS can be used to format numbers and currencies on multilingual websites and consider best practices for accommodating various localization requirements.

1. Understanding Regional Differences

Numbers and currency formats can vary significantly from one region to another. For instance, while the United States uses commas as thousands separators and periods as decimal points (e.g., 1,234.56), many European countries follow the opposite convention (e.g., 1.234,56). Additionally, the placement of currency symbols can differ.

2. CSS for Basic Number Formatting

CSS can be used to style numbers and currency symbols to match your website's design. For instance, you can define the color and font size for numbers:

```
<p class="number">$1,234.56</p>
```

```
/* Styling numbers */

.number {

font-size: 1.2rem;

color: #007bff;

}
```

While CSS can help with styling, it's important to note that CSS alone does not provide advanced number or currency formatting based on locale preferences.

3. JavaScript for Number and Currency Localization

To handle number and currency formatting that respects regional preferences, JavaScript is often employed. JavaScript's Intl.NumberFormat object allows you to format numbers and currencies based on the user's locale:

```javascript
// Using Intl.NumberFormat for currency formatting

const currencyFormatter = new Intl.NumberFormat('de-DE', {

style: 'currency',

currency: 'EUR',

});

const formattedCurrency = currencyFormatter.format(1234.56); // €1.234,56

// Using Intl.NumberFormat for number formatting

const numberFormatter = new Intl.NumberFormat('fr-FR');
```

```
const formattedNumber = numberFormatter.format(1234.56); // 1
234,56
```

In the code above, Intl.NumberFormat is used to format numbers and currencies according to the German (de-DE) and French (fr-FR) locales, respectively. This ensures that the formatting matches the preferences of users from those regions.

4. Server-Side Formatting

For server-generated content, it's common to perform number and currency formatting on the server side using server-side programming languages such as PHP, Python, or Ruby. These languages provide libraries and functions for localized number and currency formatting, ensuring consistency across the website.

5. User Preference Options

In some cases, websites may allow users to specify their preferred number and currency formats. This can be achieved by providing options in the user's profile or settings. Remember to save and apply user preferences consistently to enhance the user experience.

In conclusion, correctly formatting numbers and currencies is vital for internationalized websites. While CSS can help with styling, the actual localization of number and currency formats is typically achieved through JavaScript or server-side programming. By considering the preferences of your target audience and providing flexible formatting options, you can create a website that is inclusive and user-friendly for visitors from diverse cultural backgrounds.

Section 18.5: Cultural Considerations in Design

When designing internationalized websites, it's crucial to go beyond just language translation and consider cultural nuances and sensitivities. Cultural considerations play a significant role in how users perceive and interact with your website. In this section, we'll explore key cultural factors that web designers and developers should take into account.

1. Color Symbolism

Colors have different meanings and associations in various cultures. For example, while white may symbolize purity and innocence in Western cultures, it can represent mourning or death in some Asian cultures. Red, on the other hand, often symbolizes luck and happiness in Asian cultures but can signify danger or anger in Western cultures.

When choosing color schemes for your website, consider the cultural context of your target audience. It's advisable to research color symbolism in the regions you're targeting and choose colors accordingly.

2. Imagery and Symbols

Images and symbols can carry cultural significance. What may be considered a positive or neutral symbol in one culture could have negative connotations in another. For instance, an image of a hand gesture may be innocuous in one culture but offensive in another.

Avoid using culturally sensitive symbols or images that may inadvertently alienate or offend your audience. Conduct cultural research or consult with experts to ensure your choice of imagery is culturally appropriate.

3. Language Variations

Even within the same language, there can be significant regional variations in vocabulary, grammar, and idioms. For example, American English and British English have differences in spelling (e.g., "color" vs. "colour") and terminology (e.g., "elevator" vs. "lift").

When translating your content, consider these language variations and provide options for users to select their preferred regional dialect. It's also essential to test your content with native speakers to ensure accuracy.

4. Date and Time Formats

Date and time formats can vary widely across cultures. While the United States typically uses the month-day-year format (e.g., 10/25/2023), many other countries follow the day-month-year format (e.g., 25/10/2023).

To accommodate different date and time preferences, consider providing options for users to select their preferred formats. Use localization libraries or APIs to automatically format dates and times based on the user's locale.

5. Content Sensitivity

Content sensitivity varies from culture to culture. Humor, references to religion, politics, or controversial topics can be interpreted differently in various regions. What's considered humorous in one culture may not resonate with another.

When creating content, be aware of these sensitivities and avoid content that may be offensive or inappropriate in certain cultural contexts. Conduct cultural sensitivity training if your team is diverse or consult with experts to ensure your content is culturally respectful.

6. User Experience (UX) Considerations

Cultural considerations also extend to the user experience. Pay attention to factors like user interface design, navigation, and layout preferences that may vary among cultures. Some users may have different expectations regarding website structure and usability.

Conduct user testing with individuals from diverse cultural backgrounds to gather feedback and make necessary adjustments to your website's UX design.

In conclusion, designing for a global audience involves more than just translating content. Cultural considerations are essential for creating websites that are inclusive, respectful, and appealing to users from various cultural backgrounds. By taking the time to research and understand these cultural factors, you can enhance the user experience and ensure your website's success in international markets.

Chapter 19: CSS Debugging and Troubleshooting

In the world of web development, debugging and troubleshooting are indispensable skills. CSS, like any other programming language, can lead to issues that need to be resolved. This chapter will delve into various aspects of debugging and troubleshooting CSS, helping you identify and fix problems efficiently.

Section 19.1: Identifying and Fixing CSS Bugs

CSS bugs can manifest in various ways, from layout issues to unexpected behavior. Identifying and fixing these bugs is a fundamental skill for web developers. Here's a step-by-step guide to help you tackle CSS bugs effectively:

1. Replicate the Issue

The first step in fixing a CSS bug is to replicate it consistently. Understand the specific conditions or actions that trigger the problem. Make sure you can recreate the issue reliably in your development environment.

2. Inspect Elements with Developer Tools

Most modern web browsers come with developer tools that allow you to inspect and manipulate page elements. Right-click on the problematic element and select "Inspect" or press F12 to open the developer tools. This tool lets you see the CSS rules applied to the element, making it easier to identify conflicting styles or errors.

3. Check the CSS Rules

Examine the CSS rules that are affecting the problematic element. Look for typos, missing or incorrect property values, and syntax errors. Ensure that the rules are targeting the correct elements using selectors.

4. Check for Specificity Issues

CSS specificity determines which styles take precedence when multiple rules apply to the same element. Use the developer tools to check the computed styles and specificity of the rules. Adjust your selectors or rules if necessary to ensure the desired styles are applied.

5. Inspect Box Model Properties

Many layout issues are related to the CSS box model properties, such as margins, padding, borders, and widths. Inspect these properties in the developer tools to ensure they are set correctly and not causing unintended layout problems.

6. Use Browser Compatibility Mode

Sometimes, CSS issues are specific to certain browsers. Most developer tools allow you to switch to browser compatibility or emulation mode, which can help you identify and address browser-specific problems.

7. Test Different Scenarios

CSS bugs may behave differently under various conditions, such as different screen sizes or user interactions. Test your website under different scenarios to see if the issue is specific to certain situations.

8. Validate Your CSS

Use CSS validation tools like the W3C CSS Validator to check your stylesheets for syntax errors and potential issues. This can help catch errors that may not be immediately obvious.

9. Seek Help and Documentation

If you're unable to identify or fix the issue on your own, don't hesitate to seek help. Online developer communities, forums, and documentation can be valuable resources for troubleshooting CSS problems. Describe your issue clearly and provide relevant code snippets to get effective assistance.

10. Keep a Record

As you work on debugging and troubleshooting CSS, keep a record of the issues you encounter and the solutions you find. This can serve as a reference for future projects and help you become a more proficient developer.

Remember that CSS debugging is often an iterative process, and patience is key. Don't be discouraged by complex issues, and keep refining your skills as you gain experience in identifying and fixing CSS bugs.

Section 19.2: Browser DevTools for CSS Debugging

Browser developer tools are indispensable when it comes to debugging and troubleshooting CSS. They provide a comprehensive set of features that enable you to inspect and manipulate CSS styles, diagnose layout issues, and understand how your styles are applied to web elements. In this section, we'll explore the key features of browser developer tools for CSS debugging.

Inspecting Elements

The heart of CSS debugging with browser dev tools is the ability to inspect individual elements on a web page. You can right-click on an element and select "Inspect" or press F12 to open the developer tools. The Elements or Inspector panel will display the HTML structure of the page, allowing you to select and inspect any element.

Inspect Element

Viewing Applied Styles

Once you've selected an element, you can navigate to the "Styles" or "Computed" panel in the developer tools. This panel displays all the CSS styles applied to the selected element, including styles inherited from parent elements and user agent styles.

Applied Styles

Modifying Styles

Browser dev tools enable you to experiment with CSS styles in real-time. You can edit existing styles, add new styles, or disable styles to see the immediate impact on the selected element. These changes are temporary and do not affect the actual CSS files.

Modifying Styles

Box Model Inspection

The "Box Model" panel in the developer tools provides insights into an element's layout. It shows the dimensions, padding, margins, borders, and content area of the selected element. This is invaluable for diagnosing layout issues.

Box Model Inspection

Pseudo-Element and Pseudo-Class Inspection

If you're working with pseudo-elements (::before and ::after) or pseudo-classes (:hover, :focus, etc.), the developer tools allow you to inspect and modify their styles just like regular elements.

CSS Specificity and Inheritance

Browser dev tools display the specificity of CSS selectors, helping you understand why a particular style is applied. You can see which rules are overridden and which take precedence. This is crucial for resolving style conflicts.

Color Picker

When dealing with color-related issues, the color picker tool allows you to inspect and modify colors visually. You can pick colors from the page or modify existing color values.

Color Picker

Device Emulation

To debug responsive designs, developer tools provide device emulation modes where you can test how your page looks on different screen sizes and orientations. This is especially useful for identifying layout issues specific to certain devices.

Device Emulation

Network Tab for Loading CSS Files

If your CSS is loaded from external files, the Network tab in developer tools shows all the requests made by your page. You can inspect the loaded CSS files, check their status, and see their content for debugging purposes.

Console for CSS-Related Errors

The Console panel is useful for catching CSS-related errors and warnings. It can help you identify syntax issues, missing files, or other problems in your stylesheets.

In summary, browser developer tools are an essential companion for CSS debugging. Whether you're dealing with layout problems, style conflicts, or responsive design challenges, these tools empower you to inspect, experiment, and troubleshoot CSS effectively. By mastering these features, you can streamline your CSS development workflow and become a more proficient web developer.

Section 19.3: CSS Linting and Code Analysis

CSS linting and code analysis tools are valuable resources for maintaining code quality and consistency in your stylesheets. They help identify potential issues, enforce coding standards, and improve overall code readability. In this section, we'll explore the concept of CSS linting and the tools available for this purpose.

What Is CSS Linting?

CSS linting is the process of analyzing your CSS code to catch errors, potential bugs, and violations of coding standards. Linters are automated tools that scan your CSS files and provide feedback on areas that need improvement. They can help you find and fix common issues, maintain a consistent coding style, and ensure your code is clean and error-free.

Benefits of CSS Linting

1. **Error Detection**: Linters can identify syntax errors, typos, and incorrect CSS declarations that might otherwise go unnoticed.
2. **Coding Standards**: Linting tools enforce coding standards and best practices, ensuring that your CSS code follows a consistent style guide.
3. **Improved Readability**: Linters can highlight code that's hard to read, encouraging you to write more maintainable and understandable CSS.
4. **Performance Optimization**: Some linters can detect inefficient or redundant CSS rules that could impact page load times.
5. **Cross-Browser Compatibility**: Linting can help you avoid CSS properties or values that are not supported by certain browsers.

Popular CSS Linting Tools

1. **Stylelint**: Stylelint is a widely used CSS linter that provides a robust set of rules and plugins. It can be customized to suit your project's specific coding standards.
2. **ESLint with stylelint-plugin-css**: If you're already using ESLint for JavaScript, you can extend it to lint your CSS using the stylelint-plugin-css extension.
3. **CSSLint**: CSSLint is another popular linter with a focus on enforcing best practices and catching common CSS coding mistakes.
4. **Prettier**: While Prettier is primarily a code formatter, it

can work alongside linters to enforce code style consistency in CSS.

Setting Up and Using a CSS Linter

To get started with a CSS linter, you typically need to install it as a development dependency using a package manager like npm or yarn. Here's a basic example of setting up and using Stylelint:

 # Install Stylelint and recommended configuration

npm install stylelint stylelint-config-recommended—save-dev

Create a .stylelintrc.json configuration file with your preferred rules:

{

"extends": "stylelint-config-recommended",

"rules": {

// **Your custom rules here**

}

}

You can run the linter using the command line:

npx stylelint "**/*.css"

This command will lint all CSS files in your project.

Understanding Linter Output

When you run a CSS linter, it will analyze your CSS files and provide feedback in the terminal. It will flag any issues it finds, along with line numbers and descriptions of the problems.

Here's an example of what a linting report might look like:

/path/to/your/file.css

34:5   ✖   Unexpected   unknown   property   "dipaly"
property-no-unknown

In this example, the linter has found an error on line 34 of the CSS file. It reports that the property "dipaly" is unexpected, along with the rule that caught the error ("property-no-unknown").

Conclusion

CSS linting is a valuable practice for maintaining clean and error-free stylesheets. By incorporating a CSS linter into your development workflow, you can catch and address issues early, improve code quality, and ensure that your CSS adheres to coding standards and best practices. This ultimately leads to more maintainable and reliable CSS code.

Section 19.4: Troubleshooting Layout Issues

Troubleshooting layout issues in CSS can be a challenging but essential part of web development. Layout problems can lead to inconsistent designs, broken user experiences, and compatibility issues across different devices and browsers. In this section, we will explore common layout issues and strategies to identify and resolve them.

Common Layout Issues

1. Misaligned Elements: Elements that should be vertically or horizontally aligned may appear misaligned due to issues with margins, padding, or positioning.

2. Overflow and Scrollbars: When content overflows its container, unexpected scrollbars can appear, disrupting the layout.

3. Z-Index Problems: Elements with different z-index values can overlap incorrectly, leading to unexpected stacking orders.

4. Responsive Layout Challenges: Ensuring that your layout works well on various screen sizes and devices can be complex, resulting in issues like elements overlapping or not scaling properly.

5. Floating Elements: Floating elements can sometimes cause layout problems, especially when they are not cleared properly.

6. Empty Containers: Empty containers may collapse, affecting the layout. These can be challenging to diagnose visually.

7. Table Layout Issues: Using tables for layout can lead to unintended behavior, especially in responsive designs.

8. Inconsistent Margins and Padding: Inconsistent margin and padding values can break the alignment and spacing of elements.

Strategies for Troubleshooting Layout Issues

1. Inspecting the DOM: Use browser developer tools to inspect the Document Object Model (DOM) and see how elements are structured. *You can manipulate the DOM in real-time to test potential fixes.*

2. *Checking CSS Properties: Review the CSS properties applied to the problematic elements. Pay attention to margins, padding, positioning, and z-index.*

3. *Testing in Different Browsers: Test your layout in various web browsers to identify cross-browser compatibility issues. Browser-specific CSS can sometimes be necessary.*

4. *Using Validation Tools: HTML and CSS validation tools can help identify syntax errors and potential issues in your code.*

5. *Applying Clearfix: When dealing with floated elements, consider applying a clearfix technique to ensure that parent containers properly contain their children.*

6. *Responsive Design Testing: Test your layout on different screen sizes and devices using responsive design testing tools or by manually resizing your browser window.*

7. *Debugging Tools: Use debugging tools and techniques like adding temporary borders, backgrounds, or outlines to elements to visualize their positioning and sizing.*

Case Study: Debugging a Misaligned Layout

Let's consider a specific example: a misaligned layout where two columns are not aligning properly. By using the strategies mentioned above, you can inspect the DOM, review the CSS properties, and apply debugging techniques to identify and correct the issue.

```
<div class="container">

<div class="column1">Content in Column 1</div>

<div class="column2">Content in Column 2</div>

</div>

.container {

display: flex;

justify-content: space-between;

}

.column1 {

width: 40%;

}

.column2 {

width: 40%;

}
```

In this case, you can use browser developer tools to inspect the container, columns, and their computed styles. You might discover that margins, padding, or other CSS properties are causing the misalignment. Adjusting the CSS properties or using debugging techniques like borders can help you pinpoint and resolve the issue.

Conclusion

Troubleshooting layout issues is an essential skill for web developers. By understanding common layout problems, using debugging tools, and systematically applying troubleshooting strategies, you can identify and resolve issues that impact the visual design and user experience of your web projects. Remember that practice and patience are key to becoming proficient at layout troubleshooting.

Section 19.5: Handling Cross-Browser Compatibility Bugs

Ensuring cross-browser compatibility is a crucial aspect of web development. Different web browsers interpret HTML, CSS, and JavaScript in their ways, often leading to inconsistencies and bugs in the rendering of web pages. In this section, we will explore common cross-browser compatibility issues and strategies to address them.

Common Cross-Browser Compatibility Issues

1. CSS Rendering Differences: Each browser may interpret CSS rules differently, resulting in variations in layout, spacing, and positioning.

2. JavaScript Compatibility: JavaScript behavior can vary across browsers, causing unexpected errors or failures in functionality.

3. HTML Interpretation: Browsers may interpret HTML elements and attributes differently, leading to rendering discrepancies.

4. Unsupported Features: Some browsers may not support certain HTML5, CSS3, or JavaScript features, requiring fallbacks or alternative implementations.

5. Vendor Prefixes: Vendor-specific CSS prefixes (e.g., -webkit-,

-moz-, -ms-) are necessary for certain properties and features, but managing them can be challenging.

Strategies for Handling Cross-Browser Compatibility

1. Use Modern Web Standards: Stick to standardized HTML5, CSS3, and JavaScript features whenever possible. Modern browsers are more likely to support these standards consistently.

2. Progressive Enhancement: Start with a baseline design and functionality that works in all browsers, then enhance it for modern browsers with advanced features.

3. Feature Detection: Use JavaScript feature detection libraries like Modernizr to check for browser support before applying specific features or styles.

4. Testing on Multiple Browsers: Regularly test your website on various browsers, including both desktop and mobile, to identify and address compatibility issues early.

5. Normalize or Reset CSS: Use CSS reset or normalize stylesheets to establish a consistent baseline for browser rendering.

6. CSS Prefixes: When using CSS features with vendor prefixes, use automated tools like Autoprefixer to add prefixes automatically based on your desired browser support.

7. Polyfills: Employ JavaScript polyfills to provide support for missing features in older browsers. These polyfills replicate modern functionality.

Case Study: CSS Flexbox Compatibility

Let's consider a specific example involving CSS Flexbox, a layout model that simplifies complex layouts. While Flexbox is well-supported in modern browsers, older versions may exhibit issues. Here's a simple Flexbox layout and how you can address compatibility:

```
<div class="container">

<div class="item">Item 1</div>

<div class="item">Item 2</div>

</div>

.container {

display: flex;

justify-content: space-between;

}

.item {

flex: 1;

}
```

In this case, older versions of Internet Explorer (e.g., IE 11) may not fully support Flexbox. To address this, you can provide an alternative layout for such browsers using CSS feature detection or conditional stylesheets.

```
/* Fallback for browsers without Flexbox support */

.container {
```

```
display: block;

}

.item {

width: 50%;

float: left;

}
```

Conclusion

Cross-browser compatibility is an ongoing concern in web development. By adhering to modern web standards, employing feature detection, and using strategies like progressive enhancement and polyfills, you can create web experiences that work consistently across a wide range of browsers and devices. Regular testing and the use of tools can significantly simplify the process of handling cross-browser compatibility bugs. Remember that staying informed about browser updates and evolving web standards is essential to maintaining compatibility in the ever-changing landscape of web development.

Chapter 20: Advanced CSS Techniques

Section 20.1: CSS Custom Properties (Variables)

In this section, we'll delve into one of the most powerful features introduced in CSS: custom properties, commonly known as CSS variables. CSS custom properties allow you to define your reusable values within your stylesheets, enabling greater flexibility and maintainability in your CSS code.

What Are CSS Custom Properties?

CSS custom properties, denoted by —property-name, provide a way to store and reuse values in your CSS. They resemble traditional variables in programming languages, allowing you to define a value once and reuse it across your stylesheets.

Here's a simple example of defining a CSS custom property:

:root {

—primary-color: #3498db;

}

.button {

background-color: var(—primary-color);

color: white;

}

In this example, we've defined a custom property —primary-color within the :root pseudo-class, which represents the top-level element (usually the html element). We then use this property as the background color for a button element. If you decide to change the primary color, you can update it in one place, affecting all elements that use it.

Benefits of CSS Custom Properties

1. Reusability: As demonstrated, custom properties allow you to reuse values throughout your CSS, reducing redundancy and making your code more maintainable.

2. Dynamic Theming: You can create dynamic themes for your website by changing custom property values through JavaScript. This enables users to switch between themes easily.

3. Scoped Variables: Custom properties can be defined within specific elements or components, providing a scope for their use. This prevents unintended global changes.

4. Fallback Values: You can set fallback values for custom properties, ensuring compatibility with browsers that don't support them.

Using Custom Properties for Responsive Design

Custom properties are particularly valuable for responsive design. You can define breakpoints and other responsive values as custom properties, making it easier to manage changes for different screen sizes.

:root {

—breakpoint-medium: 768px;

```
}

@media screen and (min-width: var(—breakpoint-medium)) {

/* Styles for medium-sized screens */

}
```

Browser Support

CSS custom properties enjoy excellent browser support in modern browsers, including Chrome, Firefox, Safari, Edge, and more. However, for older browsers, such as Internet Explorer 11, support may be limited or require preprocessing with a tool like PostCSS.

Conclusion

CSS custom properties are a valuable addition to your toolkit for advanced CSS techniques. They provide a more efficient way to manage and reuse values in your stylesheets, promoting maintainability and flexibility. Whether you're building responsive designs or dynamic theming systems, custom properties can significantly enhance your CSS workflow.

Section 20.2: CSS Houdini: Extending CSS's Capabilities

In this section, we'll explore CSS Houdini, a set of emerging web standards and APIs that enable developers to extend and enhance the capabilities of CSS. CSS Houdini allows for the creation of custom CSS properties and functions, enabling a level of CSS extensibility and flexibility that was previously unavailable.

What is CSS Houdini?

CSS Houdini is a collective term for a set of APIs and technologies aimed at giving developers greater control over the CSS rendering engine. It's not a single technology but rather a combination of several specifications, each addressing a different aspect of CSS extensibility.

CSS Paint API:

The CSS Paint API, also known as the "Paint Worklet," allows developers to define custom paint functions that can be used to draw graphics in CSS properties like background-image and border-image. This opens up the possibility of creating complex patterns, gradients, and animations directly in CSS.

```
// JavaScript code defining a custom paint function

registerPaint('customPattern', class {

paint(ctx, size) {

// Paint custom pattern here

}

});
```

CSS Layout API:

The CSS Layout API, also known as "Layout Worklet," provides developers with the ability to create custom layout algorithms. This can be useful for designing complex layouts that are not easily achievable with traditional CSS layout models like Flexbox or Grid.

CSS Animation Worklet:

The CSS Animation Worklet allows for the creation of custom animations and transitions. With this API, developers can define animations using JavaScript and link them to CSS properties.

Benefits of CSS Houdini

1. Extensibility: CSS Houdini opens up CSS for extension, allowing developers to create custom CSS properties and functions tailored to their specific needs.

2. Performance: Custom paint functions can be highly optimized for performance, leading to smoother animations and reduced reliance on images.

3. Flexibility: Developers can now experiment with new CSS features and layouts that were previously impossible or difficult to achieve.

4. Polyfilling: While CSS Houdini is not supported in all browsers yet, polyfills are available to enable broader adoption and ensure compatibility.

Browser Support

CSS Houdini is an emerging technology, and browser support varies. Some features may require enabling experimental flags in browsers like Chrome. It's essential to check the current support status and keep an eye on updates as browser vendors implement these APIs.

Getting Started with CSS Houdini

To get started with CSS Houdini, you'll need a good understanding of JavaScript and CSS. You can experiment with Houdini features in modern browsers that support them or use polyfills to enable support in older browsers.

Conclusion

CSS Houdini represents an exciting frontier in web development, empowering developers to push the boundaries of what can be achieved with CSS. By creating custom paint functions, layouts, and animations, developers can craft unique and innovative web experiences. While it's still in the early stages of adoption, CSS Houdini promises to play a significant role in the future of web development, offering new levels of extensibility and creativity in CSS.

Section 20.3: CSS-in-JS: Styling with JavaScript

In this section, we will explore the concept of CSS-in-JS, a modern approach to styling web applications that involves using JavaScript to generate and manage CSS styles dynamically. CSS-in-JS has gained popularity because it offers benefits such as improved modularity, scoped styling, and enhanced developer tooling.

What is CSS-in-JS?

CSS-in-JS is an umbrella term for various libraries and tools that enable developers to write and manage CSS styles using JavaScript. Instead of writing static CSS files, developers define styles as JavaScript objects or functions, and these styles are then injected into the application's HTML during runtime.

Here are some key characteristics of CSS-in-JS:

1. Scoped Styles: CSS-in-JS encourages scoped styles by default. This means that styles are applied only to the components or elements they are intended for, reducing the risk of unintended style conflicts.

2. Dynamic Styling: Styles can be generated dynamically based on component props or application state. This makes it easy to create responsive and interactive designs.

3. Optimization: Many CSS-in-JS libraries perform optimizations, such as dead code elimination and automatic vendor prefixing, to generate efficient and production-ready styles.

4. Developer Experience: CSS-in-JS often comes with improved developer tooling, including better debugging and integration with popular JavaScript frameworks like React.

Popular CSS-in-JS Libraries

Several CSS-in-JS libraries have gained popularity within the web development community. Each of these libraries has its own syntax and features, catering to different use cases. Some of the well-known libraries include:

1. styled-components: A popular library for styling React applications, styled-components allows developers to define styles using tagged template literals.

```
import styled from 'styled-components';

const Button = styled.button`
```

```
background-color: ${props => props.primary ? 'blue' : 'white'};

color: ${props => props.primary ? 'white' : 'black'};

`;
```

2. Emotion: Another library for styling React applications, Emotion provides a flexible API for creating styled components and generating styles.

```
/** @jsxImportSource @emotion/react */

import { css } from '@emotion/react'

const buttonStyles = css`

background-color: blue;

color: white;

`;

const Button = () => (

<button css={buttonStyles}>Click Me</button>

);
```

3. Styled-jsx: This library allows developers to write scoped CSS directly in their React components using JavaScript template literals.

```
export default function Button() {

return (

<button>
```

Click Me

```
<style jsx>{`
button {
background-color: blue;
color: white;
}
`}</style>
</button>
);
}
```

Benefits of CSS-in-JS

1. Scoped Styles: CSS-in-JS naturally encourages scoped and modular styles, reducing the risk of style conflicts.

2. Dynamic Styling: Styles can be generated based on dynamic data, making it easier to create responsive designs and interactive UIs.

3. Enhanced Tooling: Many CSS-in-JS libraries offer advanced tooling and integrations with developer tools, improving the development workflow.

4. Optimizations: CSS-in-JS libraries often include optimizations that generate efficient and minimal CSS for production.

Challenges of CSS-in-JS

While CSS-in-JS offers many advantages, it's essential to consider potential challenges:

1. Learning Curve: Developers need to learn the syntax and usage of specific CSS-in-JS libraries.

2. Runtime Overhead: Generating styles at runtime can introduce some overhead, although optimizations mitigate this.

3. Tooling Compatibility: CSS-in-JS may require specific tooling and build configurations, which can be an adjustment for some developers.

Conclusion

CSS-in-JS is a powerful approach to managing styles in modern web development. It provides benefits like scoped styles, dynamic styling, and improved developer tooling. However, it's essential to choose the right CSS-in-JS library for your project and consider the learning curve and potential challenges associated with this approach. When used effectively, CSS-in-JS can lead to more maintainable and efficient CSS code in web applications.

Section 20.4: CSS Animations with GreenSock (GSAP)

In this section, we will explore GreenSock Animation Platform (GSAP), a powerful JavaScript library for creating smooth and performant animations on the web. GSAP is known for its ease of use, flexibility, and excellent performance, making it a popular choice among web developers for creating stunning animations.

What is GSAP?

GSAP, short for GreenSock Animation Platform, is a JavaScript library designed for creating animations in web projects. It offers a wide range of features and capabilities for animating HTML elements, SVG graphics, and more. GSAP is known for its simplicity and performance, making it suitable for both beginners and experienced animators.

Key Features of GSAP:

1. **Cross-Browser Compatibility**: GSAP ensures consistent animation behavior across different browsers, eliminating many cross-browser compatibility issues.
2. **High Performance**: GSAP is highly optimized for smooth animations, even on mobile devices, ensuring a delightful user experience.
3. **Tweening**: GSAP provides a powerful tweening engine that allows you to smoothly transition an element's properties over time. This includes animating properties like position, size, opacity, and more.
4. **Easing Functions**: GSAP offers a variety of easing functions to control the acceleration and deceleration of animations, creating natural motion.
5. **Timeline Control**: You can create complex sequences and timelines of animations with precise control over when animations start and overlap.
6. **Plugins**: GSAP has a vibrant ecosystem of plugins that extend its capabilities. For example, ScrollTrigger allows for animations triggered by scrolling.

Getting Started with GSAP

To get started with GSAP, you need to include the GSAP library in your project. You can do this by including the minified GSAP script in your HTML file or by installing it using a package manager like npm or yarn.

<!—Include GSAP in your HTML file—>

```
<script src="https://cdnjs.cloudflare.com/ajax/libs/gsap/3.10.1/gsap.min.js"></script>
```

Once you have GSAP included, you can start creating animations. Here's a simple example of animating an element's opacity from 0 to 1 using GSAP:

// Select the element you want to animate

```
const element = document.querySelector('.animate-me');
```

// Create a GSAP tween

```
gsap.to(element, { opacity: 1, duration: 1, delay: 0.5 });
```

In this example, we select an element with the class "animate-me" and use GSAP's to method to create a tween that animates the element's opacity to 1 over a duration of 1 second with a delay of 0.5 seconds.

Advanced GSAP Techniques

GSAP provides advanced features like creating staggered animations, controlling timelines, and using physics-based animations. It also integrates seamlessly with popular JavaScript frameworks like React and Vue.js.

Here's an example of a staggered animation using GSAP:

// Select all elements with the class "animate-item"

```
const elements = document.querySelectorAll('.animate-item');
```

// Create a timeline

```
const tl = gsap.timeline();

// Stagger the animation of elements

tl.staggerFrom(

elements,

1,

{ opacity: 0, y: 50, ease: 'power2.out' },

0.2

);
```

In this code, we select all elements with the class "animate-item" and create a timeline to control the animations. The staggerFrom method animates the elements with a staggered effect, making them fade in and move up slightly with a 0.2-second interval between each element.

Conclusion

GreenSock Animation Platform (GSAP) is a versatile and performant JavaScript library for creating animations in web development. It offers a wide range of features, excellent browser compatibility, and a straightforward API for creating animations of varying complexity. Whether you're building simple transitions or complex interactive animations, GSAP is a valuable tool in your web animation toolkit.

Section 20.5: Building a CSS Framework from Scratch

In this section, we will delve into the process of creating a CSS framework from scratch. CSS frameworks provide a set of pre-defined styles, layout structures, and components to streamline the development of web projects. By building your CSS framework, you gain a deeper understanding of CSS architecture and the flexibility to tailor styles to your project's specific needs.

Why Build Your CSS Framework?

1. **Customization**: Building your CSS framework allows you to create a style system that perfectly matches your project's design requirements. You have full control over the design decisions.
2. **Performance**: Custom-built frameworks can be optimized for performance, ensuring that your styles are efficient and load quickly.
3. **Learning Experience**: Creating a CSS framework is a valuable learning experience. You'll gain insights into CSS best practices, modular design, and maintainable code.
4. **Reusability**: Once you've developed your framework, you can reuse it across multiple projects, saving time and effort in the long run.

Steps to Build a CSS Framework

1. Define Your Design Principles

Before writing any code, establish clear design principles and goals for your framework. Consider factors like typography, color schemes, spacing, and layout structure. Having a design roadmap will guide your framework's development.

2. Organize Your Styles

Divide your styles into modular components. Create separate files for typography, colors, buttons, forms, and other UI elements. Organizing your styles helps maintain a clean and structured codebase.

3. Develop a Grid System

Grid systems are fundamental to web layout. Design and implement a flexible grid system that accommodates various screen sizes and layouts. CSS Grid or Flexbox can be powerful tools for this purpose.

4. Typography and Responsive Text

Define typography rules, including font families, sizes, line heights, and spacing. Ensure that your text is responsive, adapting gracefully to different screen sizes and orientations.

5. Create UI Components

Build reusable UI components such as buttons, forms, navigation menus, and cards. These components should be highly customizable through CSS classes or variables.

6. Handle Responsiveness

Implement responsive design principles to ensure your framework works well on devices of all sizes. Utilize media queries to adjust styles for different breakpoints.

7. Test and Debug

Thoroughly test your framework across various browsers and devices to identify and fix any compatibility issues. Use browser developer tools to debug your CSS.

8. Document Your Framework

Documentation is essential for users of your framework. Create clear and comprehensive documentation that explains how to use and customize your CSS framework.

9. Optimize for Production

Minify and compress your CSS files to reduce file size. Implement techniques like lazy loading for non-essential styles to enhance performance.

Example Code Snippets

Here are some code snippets illustrating key aspects of building a CSS framework:

```
/* Typography Styles */
body {
    font-family: Arial, sans-serif;
```

```
font-size: 16px;

line-height: 1.5;

}
/* Grid System */
.container {

max-width: 1200px;

margin: 0 auto;

padding: 20px;

}
/* Button Styles */
.button {

display: inline-block;

padding: 10px 20px;

background-color: #007bff;

color: #fff;

border: none;

border-radius: 4px;

cursor: pointer;

}
/* Responsive Design */
```

```
@media (max-width: 768px) {

.container {

padding: 10px;

}

}

/* Documentation Example */

/**

* Button Component

* Use the .button class to create a styled button.

* Example usage:

* <button class="button">Click Me</button>

*/
```

Conclusion

Building a CSS framework from scratch is a rewarding endeavor that enhances your CSS skills and provides a tailored solution for your web projects. By following best practices, organizing your code, and focusing on flexibility and customization, you can create a powerful CSS framework that accelerates your future web development efforts. Remember to document your framework comprehensively to make it user-friendly for yourself and others.

Milton Keynes UK
Ingram Content Group UK Ltd.
UKHW041823211123
432980UK00001BB/158

9 798223 825807